Bucl Lifeboats

150 years of gallantry

Nicholas Leach

Buckie lifeboat crew and personnel on board William Blannin. At the rear on the steps, left to right, wearing blue shirts are Dr Alison Douglas (Chair of Buckie Station Branch), Adam Robertson (Deputy Launching Authority) and on deck Alex Gardiner (DLA); the crew from left to right are Chris Temple, Karl Cowie, David Grant, Brian Park, Mark Herd, Jody Porter, Amanda Gardiner, Lynn Pirie, Brian Cowie, Gordon Lawtie (Second Coxswain and Mechanic), Kenny Farquhar, Mike Rennie (Deputy Coxswain), and Alan S. Robertson (Coxswain). (Nicholas Leach)

Contents

ISBN 978-0-9513656-8-7

© Nicholas Leach 2010

The rights of Nicholas Leach to be identified as the Author of this work have been asserted in accordance with the Copyrights, Designs and Patents Act 1988. All rights reserved. No part of this book may be reprinted or reproduced or utilised in any form or by any electronic, mechanical or other means, now known or hereafter invented, including photocopying and recording, or in any information storage or retrieval system, without permission in writing from the publishers.

Published by Foxglove Media

Foxglove House, Shute Hill, Lichfield, Staffs WS13 8DB

t > 01543 673594

e > foxglove.media@btinternet.com

Layout and design by Nicholas Leach

Printed by Cromwell Press Group, Trowbridge

Acknowledgements

This book could not have been written without the help and support of Adam Robertson, who answered questions, hunted out photos, and patiently answered my queries with speed and efficiency; his assistance is gratefully acknowledged, together with that of the whole of the Buckie lifeboat crew. I gladly acknowledge the work of Jeff Morris, Honorary Archivist to the Lifeboat Enthusiasts' Society, whose previous history of the station was of considerable use during the preparation of this book. The pioneering research into lifeboat history by the late Grahame Farr has also been of use. Thanks to Cliff Crone for initiating the project and supplying photographs, Andy Anderson for providing a number of old photos, and Neil Gunn, current owner of Laura Moncur, now Chizz at Lowestoft. At the RNLI, many thanks to Nathan Williams and Eleanor Driscoll for supplying images; Brain Wead and his staff for service data; and Liz Cook, Editorial Manager, for her assistance.

The lifeboat crew facility completed in 1995 with lifeboat moored nearby (not present in this photo).

The site of the lifeboat house built in 1922 for the first motor lifeboat and since demolished.

The lifeboat house built in 1885 and used until 1922.

▲ An aerial view of the town and harbour of Buckie with the various locations of the lifeboat station marked. (By courtesy of the RNLI)

▶ The unusual sight of five 17m Severn lifeboats together in Buckie harbour, with the Buckie boat on the right end. This class of lifeboat is overhauled and repaired by Buckie Shipyard Ltd. (By courtesy of Buckie RNLI)

Foreword

I feel honoured to write the foreword to this book, which provides a history of the Buckie lifeboat station and its lifeboats over the last century and a half. It also describes some of the many rescues that have been undertaken since a lifeboat was first stationed at Buckie. Many changes have taken place over the 150 years and during that time things have moved on more than anybody could have possibly imagined.

The lifeboat station at Buckie began with the willing volunteers who ran to the quayside to man the oars of the open undecked lifeboat in response to the maroons. This has progressed to the highly trained team of men and women who now crew our modern, highly sophisticated lifeboat. One thing has remained the same, however, throughout the last 150 years. Anyone finding themselves in difficulty off our coast, whatever the weather or circumstance, can be assured that the crew of the Buckie lifeboat have the same desire to render assistance and dedication to duty.

During the 150 years that Buckie lifeboat station has been in existence we have achieved a fine record of service. The crews have been awarded two Letters of Thanks Inscribed on Vellum, one Bronze medal and two Silver medals for gallantry.

Nicholas Leach has excelled in pulling together a wealth of information and facts which describe the history of the lifeboats that have served Buckie, and provided an insight into the gallant men and women who volunteer to serve the RNLI and the Buckie lifeboat. I hope you enjoy this history.

Joseph Herd
Lifeboat Operations Manager
Buckie Lifeboat

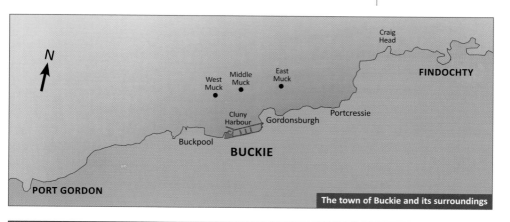

The town of Buckie and its surroundings

The first lifeboats

A lifeboat station at Buckie was established during the latter half of the nineteenth century at a time when the Royal National Lifeboat Institution (RNLI), the body founded in 1824 to organise a lifeboat service, was expanding its operations. The RNLI had been founded under the title National Institution for the Preservation of Life from Shipwreck, and during the first three decades of its existence established a number of lifeboat stations in the British Isles and Ireland. Its achievements were somewhat mixed, however, and by the 1840s its fortunes were at a low ebb with the raising of sufficient money to fund the service proving difficult. But in the 1850s a series of reforms was implemented, the service was renamed the Royal National Lifeboat Institution in 1854 and under new leadership greater revenues were generated to fund and expand the lifeboat fleet.

The Buckie station was one of several established in 1860 as the lifeboat service throughout the British Isles was greatly expanded. By the middle of the nineteenth century the town and port had expanded into one of the area's important fishing harbours, with over 1,000 fishermen employed locally. The town's large fishing fleet was often boosted by visiting fishing craft. On 6 February 1860 Commander McDonald, RN, Inspector of Coastguard for the area, wrote to RNLI Headquarters, in London, stating the need for a lifeboat station at Buckie.

In response, the RNLI's Inspector of Lifeboats, Captain J. R. Ward, visited Buckie to assess the situation, and he reported back to the RNLI on 2 April 1860 with the recommendation that a lifeboat station be established. At the next meeting of the RNLI's Committee of Management, on 5 April 1860, it was agreed that a lifeboat station be formed 'at the important fishing village

▼ Model of a 33ft self-righting lifeboat and its launching carriage dating from the early 1860s, similar to the first lifeboat which was sent to Buckie.

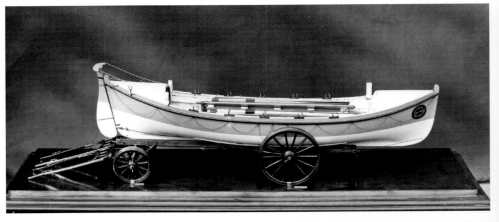

of Buckie, on the coast of Banffshire'. A week later the plans for a lifeboat house were forwarded to Banffshire and a 30ft Peake type self-righter, fitted with six oars, was ordered for the station.

The self-righter was the standard lifeboat design of the era, with similar boats being sent at the same time to Thurso and Portrush, out of a total of seventeen new lifeboats that were built by the RNLI in 1860. The boats were all constructed by the London boatbuilders Forrestt, of Limehouse, who built large numbers of these boats from the 1850s onwards.

Plans were drawn up for the building of a lifeboat house, and tenders were invited from local builders. Meanwhile, the new boat was ready by the end of October 1860 and on 26 October passed her harbour trial. Then, together with the carriage, which had been built by Robinson at a cost of £58 17s 0d, she was taken north by rail from London, arriving at Buckie on 10 November 1860. As the boathouse was not quite ready, the lifeboat spent about three months outside on her carriage under a tarpaulin on the quayside. The house was eventually completed at a cost of £140 9s 0d.

The lifeboat as well as the launching carriage were provided out of an anonymous gift to the Institution, which had been received from 'the same benevolent lady who gave the cost of the St Ives, Newquay, and Tyrella lifeboats'. The Buckie lifeboat was christened Miriam at the request of the donor. On 11 July 1861 the boat went out on exercise, and was deliberately capsized in the harbour to demonstrate her self-righting qualities.

Miriam completed three effective services during just over a decade of service at Buckie, of which two are described here. The first took place on 2 December 1867, after the sloop Hellens, of Alloa, got into difficulties in heavy seas and a severe north-easterly gale. As the sloop could not cope with the terrible conditions, signals were made to her Captain advising him to steer the vessel onto the beach, avoiding the rocks. He succeeded in getting the vessel aground a short distance offshore, and the lifeboat was then quickly launched to save the sloop's four crew.

The most notable rescue performed by Buckie's first lifeboat took place on the evening of 29 September 1868 after a number of fishing boats were caught at sea by a northerly gale. Nine boats sheltered at Craigenroan, to the east of Buckie, but they were unable to land because of the heavy seas on the shore. As number of women and children were on board the fishing boats and, with night approaching and the weather worsening, an effort was made to get them ashore in a small boat. However, only three people were brought ashore, and using the small boat again was too risky. So a message was sent to Buckie and within ten minutes of the request for assistance being received, Miriam had been

Miriam	
On station	November 1860 – 1871
Record	3 launches, 49 lives saved
Donor	Gift of an anonymous lady
Dimensions	30ft x 7ft
Type	Peake self-righter, six-oared, altered to ten oars in 1866
Cost	£156 3s 10d
Builder	1860, Forrestt, Limehouse
Disposal	Broken up 1871

pulled out of her boathouse and was 'dragged by two horses and a hundred willing hands at a rapid pace', according to the RNLI's account.

Despite the darkness, the lifeboat put out through the 'immense breakers that thundered on the beach, [that] made the launching both dangerous and difficult'. On this first launch, she brought ashore twenty people, mostly women and children, who were safely landed. The lifeboat then put to sea and saved a further fifteen fishermen, but ten men decided to remain with the boats hoping, if possible, to stop them from being driven onto the lee shore. The lifeboat, her crew and the launchers remained on the beach throughout the night in case she was needed again. In the morning, it was discovered that one of the fishing boats had drifted onto the rocks and broken up. The boat had not been manned, but, with the storm worsening, the ten fishermen who had braved the night signalled they wished to be rescued. Miriam was then launched and brought the remaining men to safety.

Coxswain james Gale's part in these rescues was particularly notable as he had been injured and badly bruised after being thrown against the side of the boat when the lifeboat was being beached after the first launch. Despite this, however, he again took the helm when the lifeboat was launched the following morning. In recognition of his courage and fine seamanship during this service, in which a total of forty-five people were rescued, the RNLI accorded him the Thanks Inscribed on Vellum.

By 1870 the RNLI had decided that a larger lifeboat, which 'was considered to be more suitable to the locality than the former boat', should be provided for the station. Ordered from Forrestt in November 1870, the new boat was a 33ft ten-oared self-righter. A new launching carriage, built by Robinson & Napton at a cost of £105 10s 0d, was also supplied. The cost of the new boat and its equipment was defrayed from a legacy left by the late James Sturm, of Holborn, after whom the boat was named.

In January 1871 the new boat and her carriage were ready. As was standard practice at the time, the railway companies 'readily gave the lifeboat a free conveyance over their lines', according to the RNLI's account. The London & North Western Railway transported her as far as Carlisle, and the Caledonian & Great North of Scotland Railway Companies the rest of the way. The new boat arrived at Portsoy, about ten miles east of Buckie, on 25 January 1871, and on her new carriage was pulled by a team of horses, loaned by Captain Hector, of Hilton, the last few miles to her new station at Buckie.

When the new lifeboat reached Buckie, 'a gratifying inauguration of the new station took place, the inhabitants, to the number of 3,000, marching out of the town in procession, headed by two bands'. The procession made its way to

James Sturm	
On station	January 1871 – 1889
Record	10 launches, 29 lives saved
Donor	Legacy of James Sturm, Holburn, London
Cost	£277 17s 6d
Dimensions	33ft x 8ft 1in
Type	Self-righter, ten-oared
Builder	1870, Forrestt, Limehouse
Disposal	Sold 1889

◄ The house built in 1885 by the harbour wall at a cost of £448. In 1907 it was altered to suit a larger 38ft Watson class lifeboat. Gas was laid on to the house in 1890 and a lantern was provided to illuminate the barometer which was mounted on the outside of the building for the use of the fishermen. This photo was taken in June 1973 and shows the building largely unaltered externally, and in use as a car repair garage. (By courtesy of Grahame Farr)

the lifeboat house, where the boat was christened James Sturm after her donor, with the Coxswain and crew later stating they were 'much pleased with their new lifeboat'.

James Sturm served at Buckie for eighteen years, during which time she undertook ten launches and saved almost thirty lives. Her first launch took place on 14 August 1874, when she went to help three fishing cobles, which were sheltering near Craigenroan in heavy seas and a north-easterly gale. The lifeboat succeeded in saving seventeen men from the cobles. However, when she was being recovered she was damaged on her port side, with the broken planks being replaced by a local boatbuilder. Further repairs were effected by a workman from Forrestt's, who was sent to Buckie in June.

Two fine services were performed by James Sturm during the first few montsh of 1876. After the schooner Claudine, of Antwerp, had been spotted off Buckie drifting, disabled and in difficulties, in heavy seas and a south-westerly gale at noon on 20 January 1876, the lifeboat was launched to help. In very cold weather, with frequent snow showers, she proceeded with a storm sail rigged, and reached the schooner nine miles offshore. Several lifeboatmen went aboard to help the schooner's crew repair some damage, and once this had been done the lifeboat returned to Buckie. She reached her station at 8am on 21 January having left two of her crew on board the schooner which, with the lifeboatmen's help, was taken into Macduff.

Within three months of going to Claudine, the lifeboat was again in action. On 11 April 1876 the schooner Elizabeth, of Llanelli, got into difficulties in heavy seas and a north-easterly gale, accompanied by heavy squalls of snow five miles east of the station. James Sturm was launched to help, and the lifeboatmen reached the casualty to find she had dropped three anchors to stop her being blown ashore, as her masts and bulwarks had carried away in the heavy weather, with huge seas pounding her. Great skill was shown by

Coxswain James Logie as he took the lifeboat, under sail, close enough to the schooner to rescue the vessel's five crew, who were safely landed at Buckie.

The Buckie lifeboatmen were involved in a long service on the morning of 15 October 1881 after a telegram had been received from the Coastguard at Portgordon, two miles to the west, stating that a vessel, flying distress signals, was drifting ashore. Pulled by a team of horses, James Sturm was taken overland on her carriage to Portgordon, where she was was successfully launched through heavy surf and into a head wind. The casualty, the schooner Equestrian, of Banff, was on passage from Dingwall to Leven. She had shipped a sea off Lossiemouth, her ballast had shifted, her sails had been blown away and she was on her beam ends by the time the lifeboatmen reachd her. The crew of four were soon taken aboard James Sturm and landed safely.

This service came at a time when the harbour was being developed and enlarged, with major changes taking place during the late 1870s and early 1880s. This affected the lifeboat's operations in a number of ways, and in April 1880 when she was taken out on exercise by the District Inspector finding a good launching place proved somewhat difficult. The usual slipway into the harbour was blocked with timber and pebbles and the boat had to be launched over the quay, which involved a drop of about eight feet. Although the lifeboat left her carriage, she also took it with her into the water, and the situation was calearly far from satisfactory. Although the carriage was recovered undamaged and the exercise was completed satisfactorily, the overall operation of the station needed to be re-examined.

▼ The boathouse built in 1885 as it is today, having been converted into a car servicing garage. Used until 1922, it remains largely unaltered externally. (Nicholas Leach)

As part of the development of Buckie during the late Victorian era, the Great North of Scotland Railway Company planned a rail link to the town in 1883. In order to extend the railway lines, the Company wanted to use the land on which the lifeboat house stood, so they contacted the RNLI with a view to purchase it. After lengthy discussions, the RNLI agreed to sell, and the Railway Company bought the boathouse and site for £121 10s 2d. The house was demolished, and to replace it a new house was built on the quayside in 1885 by W. Curamings at a cost of £447 15s 0d.

The first service by the lifeboat from the new house took place on 7 August 1887 after a pilot boat took a pilot to the schooner Ben Aigen, of Inverness, which had arrived off the port bringing coal from Sunderland. Despite the rough seas and north-westerly gale, the pilot was put aboard the schooner and the pilot boat, with one man and a young boy on board, then proceeded to return to harbour. But when the boom suddenly shifted, the pilot boat was filled with water and sank within minutes. The crew of the schooner, just fifty yards away, immediately launched their own boat which, manned by two men, rescued the man but unfortunately the boy drowned. James Sturm was launched at 9.20am, and reached the schooner's boat just in time to save the three on board, including the man from the pilot boat, before the small boat foundered on the rocks as both its oars had broken.

This proved to be the last effective service by James Sturm during her career at Bckie. Although she was called out at 1pm on 8 March 1889, after the fishing vessel Maggie Sutherland, of Findochty, had been reported in difficulties in heavy seas, the lifeboat's assistance was not needed as the vessel weathered the storm unaided. James Sturm returned to station at 3.40pm without her service being needed. Three months later she was replaced by a new lifeboat, and towards the end of the year was sold.

▼ The 35ft self-righter James Sharpe, which replaced James Sturm and served as Buckie's third lifeboat, afloat in Cullen harbour for a local flag day. (By courtesy of Andy Anderson)

James Sharpe

I n June 1887 the James Sturm lifeboat was found to be defective, but rather than repair her a new lifeboat was built for Buckie. The new boat, a standard 34ft ten-oared self-righter was ordered from D. & W. Henderson, of Glasgow, in June 1888. On 31 May 1889 she passed her harbour trial, and was sent to Buckie on 21 June 1889. She was provided out of a legacy from the late James Sharpe, of Curtain Road, Shoreditch, after whom she was named, and, like her predecessors, was launched by carriage.

The first service by the new lifeboat took place on 27 February 1890 when she launched at 5pm to assist several fishing vessels, which were attempting to enter the harbour. In heavy seas and a north-easterly gale, the lifeboat stood by until the fishing boats were safely entered port.

An incident in which the lifeboat was not involved but which proved to be a notable rescue took place on the night of 26 October 1890. The German smack Industrie was stranded near Cluny Harbour and got into severe difficulty. A number of local men, led by Peter Fernie and William Riach, waded out into the very rough seas, churned up by a strong north-easterely gale, and saved the smack's three crew. As a result of their outstanding courage, Fernie and Riach were awarded Silver medals by the RNLI, which recognised rescues even when no lifeboat was involved.

James Sharpe performed no further services for more than nine years until, on the morning of 3 November 1899, she was called out for what was a routine incident. While returning to Buckie harbour in heavy seas and a southerly gale, the lugger Welcome Home got into difficulties. One of the large fishing boats put to sea and took her in tow, and James Sharpe launched at 10.40am to stand by until the two boats had reached port.

James Sharpe was again in action in the early hours of 1 May 1900 after the lugger Mary got into difficulty. The lugger had been launched off the beach at Buckie to be taken round to Cluny Harbour to be fitted out prior to going herring fishing off the west coast. The craft was caught out by a sudden increase in the wind and a north-westerly gale creating very heavy seas. The lugger was swept past the harbour entrance forcing her crew to drop anchor. However, this failed to hold and the lugger drifted towards the rocks. James Sharpe launched at 4.45am and her crew took a spare anchor and two chains to the casualty. With the help of the lifeboat crew, the lugger was then

James Sharpe	
On station	June 1889 – 1908
Record	8 launches, 9 lives saved
Official Number	244
Donor	Legacy of J. Sharpe, Shoreditch
Cost	£441
Dimensions	34ft x 7ft 6in
Type	Self-righter, ten-oared
Builder	1888, Henderson & Co, Glasgow, yard no.He 661
Disposal	Sold 1908

The station's third lifeboat, James Sharpe, being pulled on her carriage through Cullen, a small village to the east of Buckie, for an RNLI fund-raising flag day. (Supplied by Buckie RNLI)

securely anchored and her crew of nine were landed by the lifeboat.

At 6pm on 12 April 1903 the schooner Maria, anchored in Sandend Bay, was caught out by a strong north-westerly gale, with very heavy seas and snow showers. As it was low water, launching the lifeboat near the boathouse was not possible, so she was taken two miles by road to Strathlene, launched there at 7pm and reached the casualty two hours later. The vessel was labouring heavily but not dragging her anchors, so the skipper decided to remain on board, asking Coxswain Cuthbert and his crew to stand by.

For the next three hours the lifeboat remained close to the casualty, but as the gale increased to storm force Coxswain Cuthbert requested that the skipper abandon ship. When he refused to do this, the lifeboat made for the small harbour at Portsoy, where she was moored. At about 4am on 13 April one of Maria's anchor cables parted and the vessel came ashore, becoming a total wreck, while her crew were rescued by local fishermen. The storm raged on and not until the early hours of 15 April, three days after leaving her station, was the lifeboat able to return to Buckie.

At 10.45am on 26 October 1906, as the fishing boat Granny Cornal was returning to Buckie in very heavy seas and a south-westerly gale, she was struck by an exceptionally large wave which carried away her mast. Another fishing boat took the disabled boat in tow, while James Sharpe launched at 11am to stand by as the two boats made their way back to Cluny Harbour, which was reached safely. The fifteen members of the crew, in their open lifeboat, suffered considerably from cold and exposure during this service.

This incident proved to be the last service by James Sharpe during nineteen years of service, in which she launched only eight times on service. The infrequent demand for her services – she launched only twice between 1901 and 1908 – can be put down principally to her small size. Powered by oars rather than sails, her limited range was insufficient to get to many casualties and effectively cover the seas, and, by the time of the Granny Cornal service, plans were in place to provide Buckie with a larger lifeboat.

The last pulling lifeboat

▶ The 38ft Watson sailing lifeboat Maria Stephenson inside the building hall of Thames Iron Works. (By courtesy of the RNLI)

In October 1906 the RNLI's District Inspector visited Buckie and met the local committee and Coxswain, who explained that a more powerful lifeboat was needed for the station. The service in April 1903, described above, had shown that a larger lifeboat, 'with good sailing qualities', was needed if rescues were to be carried out more effectively. The RNLI's Committee of Management agreed to this request, and so in January 1907 the Coxswain and crew visited neighbouring stations to determine the best type of lifeboat for Buckie, and requested that a Watson non-self-righting type, 38ft in length, be supplied.

At this time, more than 900 fishermen were living in Buckie and these men, some of whom formed the crew, were more familiar with sailing boats than pulling craft. As a result, the new lifeboat, which was primarily designed for sailing, was ordered from the boatyard of Thames Iron Works, at Blackwall, London, in February 1907. She was appropriated to a legacy given by the late Miss Maria Langton, of Chelsea, and was named Maria Stephenson.

To accommodate the new lifeboat, alterations

Maria Stephenson	
On station	18 January 1908 – August 1922
Record	13 launches, 13 lives saved
Official Number	581
Donor	Legacy of Miss Maria M. Langton, Chelsea
Cost	£1,120 11s 4d
Dimensions	38ft x 9ft 4in
Type	Watson, twelve-oared
Builder	1907, Thames Iron Works, Blackwall, yard no.TL21
Disposal	Transferred to Reserve 7D 12.2.1926; served at Moelfre 1929-30 and Abersoch 1930-31; sold 11.1936

were made to the lifeboat house, at a cost of £68, including the doors being widened and a capstan being provided. The launching carriage from Tenby was adapted at a cost of £60, being fitted with pushing and steering poles, while the sloping road into the harbour, down which the boat had been taken for launching, was deemed suitable to be used by the new craft.

The new lifeboat completed her harbour trial on 11 December 1907 and was handed over to the RNLI on 4 January 1908. She was forwarded to Buckie two weeks later, being brought via the London and North Western Railway and the Great North of Scotland Railway. As the crew had requested, the new boat was a 38ft by 9ft 4in Watson class, pulling twelve oars with a No.1 sailing rig, and had cost £1,120 11s 4d to build. Unusually, she was fitted with a steering wheel as the Coxswain and crew were 'more accustomed to steer with a wheel than any other form of steering gear'.

Maria Stephenson was christened on 24 March 1908 by Mrs Campbell, and after the ceremony the lifeboat was 'launched and manoeuvred off the harbour under sail and oars' to prove her capabilities to the assembled crowd. She served at Buckie for fourteen years, during which time she launched thirteen times on service and is credited with saving thirteen lives. Her first launch was on 8 June 1908 when she went to the aid of the fishing vessel Speedwell, of Wick, but her services were not required so she returned to station.

The first effective service by Maria Stephenson took place on 16 March 1909, when she was launched at 5.50pm after the fishing boat Superb, of Portessie, had lost her mast in heavy seas five miles offshore. The lifeboat was sailed to the casualty, which was rolling heavily in the rough seas. A tow line was secured and the fishing boat was brought into harbour.

Later in the same year she was out again, on the morning of 5 October 1909, after the fishing boat The Boy, of Findochty, got into difficulties about four miles north-east of Buckie Harbour. The boat's sail had been carried away in rough seas and a southerly gale, and the sole occupant was seen waving

◀ Maria Stephenson on her launching carriage on the slipway into Buckie harbour. (Supplied by Buckie RNLI)

to indicate he needed assistance. Maria Stephenson launched just before midday, headed out to the casualty, and found the owner, a man of nearly seventy, exhausted. He was taken on board the lifeboat and the lifeboatmen secured a line to his boat, which was towed to Findochty Harbour.

Maria Stephenson was launched at 10.30am on 19 April 1911 after the small boat Joseph, of Banff, with three crew on board, was seen flying a distress signal six miles north of Buckie. The casualty had lost her sails and rudder in the bad weather. Once on scene, the lifeboat took Joseph in tow, with Coxswain Cuthbert taking Maria Stephenson four miles to the west to check on a number of small fishing boats which were trying to return to harbour. After standing by until all of them were safe, the lifeboat towed Joseph into Buckie harbour.

What proved to be the last service launch by Maria Stephenson, and also the last launch by a pulling and sailing lifeboat at Buckie, took place on 13 February 1920. The lifeboat put out at 12.15am to the motor boat Loyal, of Buckie, but her services were not needed and so she was rehoused at 4am.

By this time, plans were afoot to station a motor lifeboat at Buckie, and problems had been experienced with launching using the carriage. In December 1921 the carriage had stuck in mud during a launch, and so the lifeboat could not reach the casualty. As a result, it was decided that Maria Stephenson should be kept afloat until the new lifeboat arrived.

Maria Stephenson left Buckie on 29 July 1922 and was sent to the RNLI's storeyard, at which point she was transferred to the Reserve Fleet. She went on to serve at Moelfre from September 1929 to 1930, and then was operated at Abersoch from 1930 to 1931. She was then sold out of service in November 1936 for £130 to A. C. Crocket, of Pulborough in Sussex, but her whereabouts since being sold are unknown.

▼ Maria Stephenson being recovered, with her carriage being hauled out of the water. (By courtesy of Buckie RNLI)

The first motor lifeboat

◀ The station's first motor lifeboat was K. B. M., a 40ft Watson motor which cost £8,000 to build. The new boathouse cost £15,000, making a total of £23,000 for one station. Buckie was the ninth out of forty-four Scottish stations then operational to be equipped with a motor lifeboat. She is pictured under sail, as she carried auxiliary sails in case her engine failed. (By courtesy of Buckie RNLI)

The first motor lifeboat to serve at Buckie came to the station in August 1922. The RNLI had been developing motor lifeboats since the early years of the twentieth century, but the First World War had delayed the build programme and considerably slowed further advances with engines. In the immediate post-war years, however, efforts were made to catch up and a series of new motor lifeboat designs was introduced. With their greater range, motor craft could cover far greater distances than their pulling and sailing counterparts, and one motor lifeboat could effectively replace two or more pulling boats, so inevitably some stations were closed. In 1919 a decision was taken to supply a motor lifeboat to Buckie, as the town was, according to the RNLI's assessment, 'one of the chief centres of the Scotch fishing industry', and therefore a motor lifeboat was necessary.

During 1920 work started at the yard of J. S. White on the construction of the new craft for Buckie. She was a 40ft Watson class non-self-righter, one of two such boats completed in 1922, and her single 45bhp Tylor JB.4 four-cylinder petrol engine gave a top speed of 7.36 knots, developing 924rpm. Her hull form was essentially the same as the Watson sailing lifeboats, and indeed she carried sails, but her main form of power was her engine.

To accommodate the new lifeboat a new boathouse was built. Because room in the harbour at Buckie was so tight, a conventional boathouse with a roller slipway could not be built. To overcome this difficulty, the new house had an internal platform, or cradle, which supported the lifeboat. In order to launch the lifeboat, the platform would be lowered by hoists so that the boat was in a position to either float or slip into the water, depending on the state of the tide. The building, which took up less room than a conventional slipway, cost approximately £15,000 to build and was one of only two such structures constructed for the RNLI; the other was built at Sunderland.

The new lifeboat sailed from Cowes, where she had been built, on 29 July 1922 and arrived at Buckie early in August after a long passage up the east coast. The boat, which cost £8,179 to build, had been funded from three legacies which, with the consent of the executors, were amalgamated to give the unusual name K. B. M. The legacies came from the late William Kirkhope, of Edinburgh; the late Charles Bailey, of Brighton; and the late Miss Charlotte McInroy, of Bridge of Allan. The donors' full names were inscribed on a plaque fixed inside the boat.

The official naming ceremony of K. B. M. was held during spring 1923. The Duke of Richmond and Gordon, Lord Lieutenant of Banffshire, was to have presented the boat to the RNLI on behalf of the three donors, but was unable to do so due to illness, so Sir William Martin, JP, the Institution's former Organising Secretary for Scotland, stood in. In his speech Sir William spoke of the considerable increase in the cost of lifeboats and the general expenses as motorisation took over. The new boat was received by Provost Shearer, who presented her to Captain Charles Malcolm, Chairman of the Buckie Committee. After she had been dedicated by the Rev John Greenlaw, Miss Gordon, of Cairnfield, named her K. B. M.

During the ceremony, Sir William made an appeal to 'men and women of all classes' to continue funding the service, and also somewhat unusually directly to the owners and crews of the fishing fleets. Between 1919 and 1922 almost a half of the services performed by the lifeboats had been to trawlers and drifters, yet 'in spite of the large fortunes made out of the fishing industry', the contributions made by it to the RNLI were 'entirely inadequate'. Sir William believed that 'every crew should consider it a first duty to make a joint contribution each time that they returned to harbour with a good catch.'

K. B. M. served at Buckie for twenty-seven years, during which time she completed more than sixty services and gave her crew excellent service. Her first service launch came on 18 December 1922, before she had been christened, when she went out at 10.50am to assist the steam drifter Victory, of Portgordon, which had run aground on the Mid Muck Rocks, to the north-east of Buckie harbour, in moderate seas and a south-easterly gale. The drifter was towed clear by three other drifters,

K. B. M.	
On station	August 1922 – 25 Nov 1949
Record	62 launches, 12 lives saved
Official Number	681
Donor	Combined legacies of William Kirkhope, Edinburgh; Charles Chetwode Bailey, Brighton; and Miss Charlotte G. C. McInroy, Bridge of Allan.
Cost	£8,179 5s 0d
Dimensions	40ft x 11ft
Type	Watson motor
Builder	1922, J. S. White, Cowes, yard no.W1572
Disposal	Transferred to Reserve Fleet 11.1949; sold 9.1936 for £750

while the lifeboat stood by until all the vessel was safe.

The next service by K. B. M. came on 14 November 1926, when she launched at 9.20am after signals of distress had been seen about ten miles north of Buckie. The motor vessel St Blane, of Glasgow, had engine failure so the lifeboat launched to assist. Once on scene, the lifeboatmen communicated with the captain who requested that they return to port, inform the boat's owners of the breakdown, and arrange for a tug to tow the vessel to safety. This was done and the vessel was brought to safety.

Another routine service was undertaken on 27 February 1927. In the evening the steam trawler Merleton, of Granton, stranded off the village of Findhorn after being caught in thick fog. K. B. M. was soon launched and reached the casualty at 2pm. She stood by the trawler for several hours until eventually passing a wire rope and hawsers from the vessel to a steam drifter, which pulled Merleton clear at high tide. The trawler was able to proceed without further assistance, so the lifeboat returned to station.

Almost ten years passed before K. B. M. completed another effective service, although in 1934 she had been called out but was unable to complete the service. She launched at 9.30pm on 9 November to go to the motor vessel Ebenezer, of Banff, which was in difficulties having been caught out in rough seas. However, as the lifeboat made her way out to the casualty, a rope fouled her propeller and she was unable to proceed. The Whitehills and Fraserburgh lifeboats were launched to help, while the Buckie crew were forced to raise the sails, carried in case the engine failed, and make their way back to Buckie. The fishing boat also reached harbour safely, and so the other two lifeboats returned to their stations.

▼ The unique boathouse built close to the harbour entrance in 1922 for the station's first motor lifeboat. (By courtesy of the RNLI)

On 26 January 1937 K. B. M. was involved in a medical evacuation after the steam trawler Sangarius, of Aberdeen, requested medical assistance to treat an injured man on board. The lifeboat launched at 3.15pm with two doctors on board. Conditions were very bad with a heavy swell, south-easterly gale and heavy snow. As the lifeboat battled her way out to the casualty, she was struck by a very heavy wave and crew member G. Thomson sustained a badly injured knee. The doctors treated him as best they could in the difficult circumstances, despite huge seas continuing to engulf the lifeboat as she made passage towards the trawler.

Once the lifeboat had reached Sangarius, Coxswain James Goodbrand manoeuvred K. B. M. alongside with great skill, and the two doctors were transferred across to treat the injured man. As soon as his condition had been fully assessed, he was taken aboard the lifeboat, together with the doctors, and brought ashore at Buckie at 3.45pm, with the lifeboat not being rehoused until 10pm. As a result of the accident during the outward passage, crew member Thomson was permanently disabled and was subsequently granted an allowance by the RNLI.

During the Second World War the demands on the lifeboat service as a whole increased and lifeboats and their volunteer crews faced different and difficult challenges. These included operating in mine-infested waters, night-time services without guiding lights, and the danger of attack by enemy aircraft. In the north-east of Scotland, Buckie lifeboat was busier than she had ever been, and, during the conflict, answered a total of thirty-one calls and was credited with saving nine lives. The first call came on 13 November 1939, after the crew of an aircraft had been reported as having fired distress flares, but, despite a thorough search, nothing was found.

On 25 March 1941 K. B. M. was launched after an aircraft crashed into the sea off Garmouth. She put out at 2am and, in rough seas and a north-

▼ The unusual boathouse built in 1922 stood adjacent to the westernmost pier of the harbour, parallel to a timber jetty, which is still in existence. (By courtesy of the RNLI)

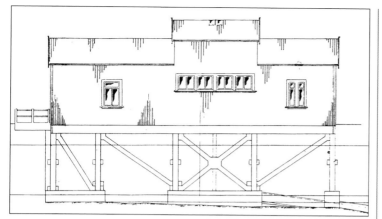

◀ Diagram of the unusual lifeboat house and its internal launching cradle built in 1922. The house was supported on concrete piles which raised it well above the high water level. The lifeboat was raised and lowered on a cradle supported on chains. (By courtesy of the RNLI)

westerly wind, the lifeboat crew found the body of an airman tied to a float, so they recovered the body and brought it ashore at Buckie. At daybreak, the lifeboat put to sea again to search for wreckage from the plane. Some more pievces were brought ashore for identification, and when K. B. M. returned to her station she had been at sea for almost eight hours.

During 1942 Buckie's lifeboatmen were kept busy, going to the aid of a variety of vessels throughout the year. The first service came on 7 March when K. B. M. launched at 6.30am after a vessel had been seen signalling for help. The lifeboatmen found HM trawler Sheldon aground on the landward side of Craigenroan Rock, but nobody on board. They heard shouts coming from the shore, and found that the trawler's crew had managed to scramble to safety. The lifeboat returned to the trawler, turned off a searchlight that had been left on, and returned to station at 7.45am. Half an hour later K. B. M. went back to the trawler after an officer asked for assistance in recovering some confidential papers and the crew's clothes from the vessel.

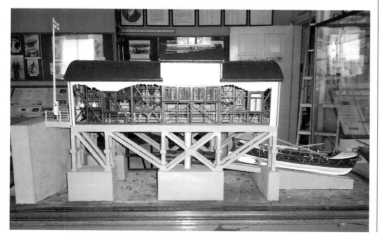

◀ Model of the 1922 lifeboat house on display in the lifeboat museum at Redcar. This clearly shows the launching cradle supported on chains, the concrete piles, and the south side of the building has been cut away to show inside the house itself. The lifeboat in the model is K. B. M. ready to be launched. (By courtesy of Buckie RNLI)

The officer was put back onto the stranded trawler, where he collected the papers and the clothes, and was then brought back to Buckie.

K. B. M. was in action again just five days later. She launched at 11.30pm to a trawler in difficulty to the north-west of the harbour. In choppy seas, a strong southerly wind and frequent snow showers, the lifeboatmen found the Fraserburgh drifter Morning Rays towing the Buckie drifter Amity, which had nobody on board. However, the tow-line had fouled Morning Rays' propeller and both vessels were drifting. The lifeboatmen helped another drifter, Copieux, take the stranded drifters in tow and escorted them towards Buckie. The tow line from Morning Rays to Amity broke at one point and had to be reconnected, and eventually all the vessels reached harbour.

An excellent rescue was completed on 15 September 1942 after RAF High Speed Launch No.170 went aground on rocks below Buckie Coastguard Station. K. B. M. launched at 9.30pm into a dark but clear night, with heavy seas and a strong squally westerly wind. The lifeboat reached the casualty ten minutes after launching and, with the coastguard's Aldis Lamp illuminating the scene from the shore, the lifeboatmen saw waves breaking over its stern and the ten crew huddled together towards the bow. The Coastguard Life-saving Team had already got a line aboard and, as they were attempting to take the men off by breeches buoy, the lifeboat waited to see if further help was needed. After the considerable danger in using the breeches buoy were evident when the first man was hauled ashore, through heavy seas and across sharp rocks, the rest of the crew requested the lifeboat be used.

So Coxswain Francis Mair took the lifeboat towards the launch's stern, but she was swept past by the strength of the wind, sea and tide and so he had to bring her round again. But just as she reached the launch again, a huge sea caught the lifeboat and pushed her rapidly towards rocks. The lifeboat crashed heavily onto the rocks and one of the lifeboatmen was thrown overboard. Coxswain Mair immediately shouted 'full astern' and the lifeboat pulled clear, after which the man thrown overboard was quickly picked up.

▶ K. B. M. served Buckie for more than twenty-seven years. During her career, she was fitted with various additional pieces of equipment. These included, in April 1941 a Phillips wireless receiver and in October the same year a mast-head hoop to take a morse signalling lamp. Significant improvements in communication equipment were made during the inter-war years. (By courtesy of Buckie RNLI)

◄ Coxswain Francis Mair and the Buckie lifeboat crew standing outside the 1922 boathouse. On Coxswain Mair's right is mechanic Charles Brown, and other members of the crew pictured are Jack Cole (back row, second right) and James Clark (front row, far right). Charles Brown was appointed Mechanic when K. B. M. first arrived in July 1922 and served in the post until April 1941, when he was succeeded by Alex Scott.

However, as the lifeboat went astern, a line which had been fired from the shore wrapped round her propeller and the engine stopped. It was restarted and, luckily, the line snapped, thus freeing the propeller. Coxswain Mair then took the lifeboat to windward of the casualty, dropped anchor, and the lifeboat was veered down towards the launch. But again she struck the rocks and had to move out into deeper water.

The anchor cable was transferred to the lifeboat's stern and Coxswain Mair took her in again, bow first. This time the lifeboat got close enough for a grappling hook to be thrown aboard the launch, but the lifeboat was directly over the rocks and each time the waves receded she came down on them. Despite the risk that the lifeboat might be smashed to pieces in this operation, Coxswain Mair took the lifeboat closer and closer to the launch until the remaining nine men could jump across to the lifeboat. The lifeboat's anchor cable was then hauled in and, by skilful use of the engine, K. B. M. was brought clear of the rocks.

Coxswain Mair set course for the harbour knowing that the lifeboat had been seriously damaged. The boat reached port safely and landed the rescued men at 10.38pm. It was only when the lifeboat was rehoused that the extent of the damage was revealed. In several places the bottom had been stove in, and apart from the engine room the whole boat was flooded. She had been kept afloat only by the air cases. For his skill and outstanding seamanship during the rescue, the RNLI accorded Coxswain Mair the Thanks on Vellum, with additional monetary awards going to the rest of the crew.

K. B. M. was repaired and once the work had been completed she was back in action. On 23 October she was called out to escort HM Drifter Archimedes, which was towing the disabled fishing boat Vesterland. The last service of the year again involved the fishing vessel Vesterland. In heavy seas and a north-easterly gale, on 29 December 1942, the vessel was attempting to enter harbour even though several other fishing boats had made for the Moray Firth to seek shelter. K. B. M. launched at 2.45pm and stood by until the fishing vessel eventually reached harbour safely at 6pm.

The last war service was undertaken on 12 January 1945, when K. B. M. was launched after an aircraft had crashed into the sea off Lossiemouth, but the lifeboat crew found only wreckage. The first service of peacetime was also to a naval craft. At 9.30pm on 8 February 1946 K. B. M. launched into rough seas and a north-westerly gale to help the Admiralty motor fishing vessel No.1067. At the request of the vessel's skipper, the lifeboat returned to harbour to arrange for tug assistance, but a destroyer assisted the casualty with the lifeboat standing by. At dawn the next day a line was passed from the destroyer to the casualty, but, while helping, the lifeboat's propeller was fouled on this line. Fortunately, the lifeboatmen were able to clear it, but the propeller had been damaged and the shaft bent. As the casualty was in no immediate danger, the lifeboat returned to Buckie and was immediately taken to the local boatyard to be repaired.

On 6 April 1946 K. B. M. helped the crew of the Danish fishing vessel Bent Eric, whcih hads ran aground on Covesea Skerries. The lifeboat launched at 5pm into choppy seas and a strong westerly wind, and reached the stranded vessel just over two hours later. The vessel, which had five crew on board, was hard aground and, as the water was too shallow for the lifeboat to get alongside, the Danish skipper was taken off, leaving two crew in the ship's small boat. At the skipper's request, the lifeboat towed the this boat to windward and then cast it adrift so that it would be blown down to the fishing boat, and its two occupants could be rescued. But the small boat was lost from sight and a prolonged search by the lifeboat failed to find it. The boat, with the two men still on board, was eventually picked up thirty-five hours later by another Danish fishing boat having drifted eastward to within five miles off Peterhead. When the tide rose, K. B. M. got alongside Bent Eric and take off the two men, and then returned to station.

The next and, as it turned out, final service by K. B. M. proved to be a challenging rescue. In the early hours of 8 January 1949 the Swedish steamer Frej, on passage from Narvik to Workington, ran into extremely heavy seas and a north-easterly gale. She sought shelter in Banff Bay and dropped two anchors. At 6.20am one of the anchor cables parted and, with the vessel now in danger, Whitehills lifeboat was alerted. But the very heavy seas, combined with dead low water, made it impossible to launch at Whitehills, so the Buckie crew was alerted.

K. B. M. got away at 8.25am and reached Frej three hours later, after an extremely rough passage. The steamer was then only just over a mile offshore and being driven steadily towards the lee shore. The lifeboat stood by for a while and then the steamer's captain asked for the majority of the crew to be taken off. It took great skill to manoeuvre the lifeboat alongside the steamer in the very rough seas, and a total of seven runs had to be made during which nineteen men were taken off. The lifeboat was damaged during the rescue, and with the survivors on board made for Buckie, where they arrived at 3.30pm after another extremely rough passage.

Meanwhile, the lifeboatmen at Whitehills, who had been standing by waiting for an opportunity to launch, were able to put to sea at 12.30pm when the weather had improved and the 35ft 6in single-engined self-righter William Maynard, on temporary duty at Whitehills, set off. The Whitehills lifeboatmen fired a line across to the remaining men on board Frej, but they decided to remain on board and wait for a tug which was on its way.

At the request of the steamer's captain, the Whitehills lifeboat stood by until 7.30pm and then put into Macduff Harbour, for fuel and for her crew to have a hot meal. She later returned to Frej and stood by until the steamer had been taken in tow by the tug. William Maynard finally returned to station at 3pm on 9 January, more than twenty-six hours after she had been launched. In gratitude for this service, the Swedish Lifeboat Society awarded a Plaque of Merit to the RNLI, and a Diploma to each of the stations involved.

By the time of this incident K. B. M. had been at Buckie for more than twenty-seven years and a new boat was being built for the station. K. B. M. left the station on 25 November 1949 with a fine record of service and was placed in the Reserve Fleet for a further three years before being sold out of service. She was bought in September 1952 by a Norfolk-based man but ended up, after being converted into a pleasure boat, on Ireland's south coast as the yacht Striker. During the early years of the twenty-first century, under new ownership, she reverted to her lifeboat name.

▼ After being sold out of service in September 1952, K. B. M. was converted into a pleasure boat and renamed Striker. She is pictured at Kinsale in August 2003 after she had her lifeboat name reinstated. (Nicholas Leach)

Glencoe, Glasgow

▶ 41ft Watson motor lifeboat Glencoe, Glasgow, pictured during trials. She served at Buckie for only eleven years having been built by Morgan Giles, one of only a handful of lifeboats built at the South Devon yard. (By courtesy of the RNLI)

The unique boathouse and launching cradle system employed at Buckie was the main consideration when determining the size and type of the next lifeboat, which had to be suitable for the building. So, to replace the 40ft Watson, a 41ft Watson was allocated to the station. This boat was similar in design to her predecessor, but was slightly larger and heavier, and was also more powerful. She was powered by two 35bhp Weyburn AE.6 six-cylinder petrol engines which gave the boat a top speed of 7.61 knots and a cruising speed of seven knots. At her cruising speed she had a radius of action of seventy-seven nautical miles.

In 1963 she was re-engined with two 47hp Parsons Porbeagle diesels, the main benefit of which was an increase in the range at which she could operate. The new boat was built by Morgan Giles, at Teignmouth, and her £11,885 cost came out of a legacy from the late Mrs Lawrence Glen. The new boat was completed in 1949 and sailed for her station towards the end of the year, arriving at Buckie on 25 November 1949.

The new lifeboat was formally named Glencoe, Glasgow at a ceremony in Buckie harbour on 29 July 1950. William Smith, JP, chairman of the

Glencoe, Glasgow	
On station	25 Nov 1949 – 30 June 1960
Record	27 launches, 9 lives saved
Official Number	857
Donor	Legacy of the late Mrs Lawrence Glen, Glasgow
Cost	£11,885 4s 8d
Dimensions	41ft x 11ft 8in
Type	Watson motor
Builder	1949, Morgan Giles, Teignmouth
Disposal	Served in Reserve Fleet 1960-65, Portavogie 1965-78; sold 1979

branch, oversaw proceedings, during which Brigadier J. W. H. Gow handed the lifeboat to the Institution on behalf of the donor, and she was accepted by Lord Saltoun, a member of the Committee of Management and a vice-president of the Scottish Lifeboat Council.

Lord Saltoun in turn handed her to the Buckie station branch, on whose behalf she was received by ex-Provost W. J. Merson, a vice-president of the branch. Rev John Greenlaw, of the North Church, Buckie, led the service of dedication, after which Colonel Sir George W. Abercromby, Lord Lieutenant of Banffshire, invited Miss M. Glen Pettigrew to name the lifeboat.

Glencoe, Glasgow spent less than twelve years at Buckie, during which time she saved nine lives. Her first effective service took place on 27 December 1951, when she launched at 3.40pm to go to the fishing vessel Cloud, of Horeman, which was ashore half-a-mile north-west of Covesea lighthouse. The lifeboat stood by until the casualty, with two crew aboard, refloated at high tide. It was then towed back to harbour by another fishing vessel and the lifeboat left the scene.

Further routine services followed, with the lifeboat launching in March 1953, with neighbouring lifeboats from Banff and Whitehills, to help search for the wreckage of a Firefly aircraft, and putting out on the afternoon of 9 May 1954 to save two youths who had got into difficulties while out in a small sailing dinghy three miles north-west of Buckie. In choppy seas and a strong south-easterly wind, the lifeboat rescued the youths and their boat was then towed back to harbour during the late afternoon.

In worsening weather on the evening of 20 January 1956, the fishing vessel Katreen broke down and was taken in tow by the local fishing vessel Briarbank. Conditions were very bad as they approached the harbour and so,

▼ The twin-engined 41ft Watson motor Glencoe, Glasgow was Buckie's second motor lifeboat. (By courtesy of the RNLI)

► Glancoe, Glasgow in the harbour shortly after launching on service to the fishing boat Elm Grove, of Buckie, on 26 February 1958 after one of the boat's crew had fallen overboard. (By courtesy of the RNLI)

at 9.37pm, Glencoe, Glasgow was launched. The sea had become extremely rough, whipped up by a north-westerly gale. The lifeboat reached the two fishing vessels within minutes, but Katreen had run onto the rocks to the north-west of the Pier as the tow line had parted. The crew of five had been taken aboard Briarbank, whose steering-gear then failed. The lifeboatmen put a tow line aboard Briarbank, with the intention of towing the disabled vessel into the harbour. But the line quickly parted and so the skipper turned the fishing vessel using just the engines, and headed out to sea to ride out the storm in the bay. The lifeboat returned to the harbour at 11.15pm. She put to sea again at 11.32am the next day as the wind had eased and escorted Briarbank into the harbour.

Having not performed any effective services during 1957, in February 1958 Glencoe, Glasgow was comparatively busy, launching three times on service. On the morning of 5 February she stood by the steamer Orkney Trader, of Kirkwall, which was in danger of coming ashore in heavy seas and a severe northerly gale with heavy snow. A fortnight later the lifeboat launched to the fishing vessel Seaforth, of Inverness, which had run aground half-a-mile north-east of Buckie harbour. In rough seas and a strong westerly wind, the lifeboat crew, using the lifeboat's searchlight, saw five of the fishermen on a life raft. They were quickly taken aboard Glencoe, Glasgow, and the lifeboatmen then searched the area for the sixth member of the fishing vessel's crew. He had been washed overboard when the boat had struck the rocks and unfortunately was never found.

On 26 February Glencoe, Glasgow was called out again to take a doctor to the fishing vessel Elm Grove, of Buckie, after one of her crew had fallen overboard. He was unconscious when pulled out of the sea, so the doctor went aboard the fishing vessel, twelve miles north-east of Buckie, but the man was dead so the lifeboat escorted Elm Grove back to Buckie.

Glencoe, Glasgow undertook the last two effective service launches of her time at Buckie during 1959. On 13 January she helped to search for an aircraft which had crashed into the sea just north of Scaur Nose Head. Several other aircraft and a helicopter were involved in the search, but only pieces of wreckage and clothing were found, and these were landed when the lifeboat returned to station at 4.45pm. On the evening of 19 March 1959 she went to the local motor boat Rosaline, which had gone aground. Once on scene, the lifeboatmen passed a tow line across to the two men on the motor boat, which was then pulled clear and taken to Buckie harbour.

By the late 1950s major problems were being experienced with the boathouse, and launching at low water was getting increasingly difficult because of a lack of depth of water caused by silting in the harbour around the building. As a result, a decision was taken in December 1959 to relocate the station, and a berth was found in No.4 Basin, at the eastern end of the harbour close to the boatyard. The new location and berth, suitable for a larger and more powerful lifeboat, has been in use ever since.

Glencoe, Glasgow launched for what proved to be the last time while at Buckie on 8 June 1960. She put out at 1.10am to the motor boat Braeraar, of Sandend, but was recalled soon after setting out as the motor boat was safe. At the end of the month she left Buckie and was reallocated to the Reserve Fleet, serving temporarily at Girvan, Port Erin, Arklow, Troon and Wicklow during the 1960s. Between 1965 and 1978 she was stationed at the Cloughey-Portavogie station in Northern Ireland, and in 1979 she was sold out of service.

▼ After service at Buckie, Girvan and Portavogie, Glencoe, Glasgow was sold out of service in March 1979 for £7,000 and converted into the pleasure boat Vagrant. Since the early 1990s she has been kept at Burghead harbour. (Nicholas Leach)

The replacement boat at Buckie was the 45ft 6in Watson H. C. J., which had been built in 1928 and stationed at Thurso for twenty-seven years. While at Buckie she undertook a couple of services. The first was on 31 August 1960, when she was called out in the early morning on a fruitless search for an aeroplane which had been reported missing, and the second was on 19 September when she went to a fishing vessel, but was recalled without her services being needed.

A few days later, H. C. J. was replaced by another reserve 45ft 6in Watson, W. & S., which had been built in 1931 and served at Penlee for almost thirty years. She launched three times during her time at Buckie, all routine services. Her first launch was on 1 October 1960 after the Sea School Training Vessel Radium, of Aberdeen, had developed engine trouble and was drifting in choppy seas. The disabled vessel was towed into Buckie just before midnight.

Laura Moncur

▶ Laura Moncur at moorings in Buckie harbour during the 1960s when her cuperstructure was painted grey. She served the station for twenty-three years. (By courtesy of Buckie RNLI)

The 45ft 6in Watson lifeboats sent to Buckie in the late 1950s and early 1960s were temporary allocations while a new lifeboat was built for the station. The new boat was a 47ft Watson non-self-righter ordered from the Cowes boatyard of Groves & Guttridge in September 1959, with a similar boat ordered at the same time from the same yard for Buckie's neighbouring station at Whitehills. Work began on the new boat in April 1960 and a year later she was ready for service.

Fitted with two 60hp Gardner 5LW diesel engines, the new lifeboat had a top speed of 8.85 knots and a cruising speed of seven and a half knots. She had a radius of action of 135 nautical miles at full speed and 270 nautical miles at cruising speed. She carried a total of 160 gallons of fuel, and was manned by a crew of eight. The boat cost £35,636 15s 8d, which was provided from the legacy of the late Miss Laura Moncur, of Edinburgh, and a gift from Miss Jessie Bridie Moncur, Mayor of Skelmorlie, together with RNLI Funds. Named Laura Moncur after the principal donor, she arrived at Buckie in June 1961 after a passage north from her builder's yard on the Isle of Wight. Her first call came in the afternoon of 21 July 1961 when she searched for a missing aircraft, but was recalled when the plane was found to be safe.

The new lifeboat was named on 25 August 1961 at a ceremony in Cluny Harbour at Buckie. William Smith, chairman of the branch, was in the

Laura Moncur	
On station	June 1961 – April 1984
Record	66 launches, 39 lives saved
Official Number	958
Donor	Legacy of Miss Laura Moncur of Colinton, Edinburgh; gift from Miss Jessie Bridie Moncur, of Skelmorlie; and RNLI funds
Cost	£35,636 15s 8d
Dimensions	47ft x 13ft
Type	Watson cabin motor
Builder	1961, Groves & Guttridge, Cowes, yard no.G&G 588
Disposal	Served in Relief 1984-88, sold out of service November 1988

◄ On 14 July 1961 the Whitehills and Buckie lifeboat stations were honoured by a visit from HM The Queen, Patron of the RNLI. Her Majesty inspected both lifeboats and met crews and officials from both stations. She is pictured at Buckie speaking to John Innes, with Jack Cole, James Roy and James Murray. (By courtesy of John Innes)

chair, and Lord Saltoun, a Vice-President of the RNLI and Convener of the Scottish Lifeboat Council, formally handed the boat over to the branch. She was accepted by Dr P. Reid, the branch's vice-chairman, with the service of dedication, conducted by the Rev J. D. Henderson of North Parish Church, following. At the end of the ceremony, the boat was christened Laura Moncur by Lady Saltoun.

Laura Moncur served at Buckie for more than twenty years, during which time she saved thirty-nine lives. Her first effective service took place on 18 August 1962. Early in the afternoon an aircraft crashed into the sea two miles off Lossiemouth and so Laura Moncur put out. A helicopter was also called out, but only pieces of wreckage were recovered, and these were landed at Lossiemouth by the lifeboat.

▼ Laura Moncur during her naming ceremony at Cluny Harbour, with the old boathouse in the background. (By courtesy of John Innes)

▶ Miss Heather Innes, daughter of bowman John Innes, presenting Lady Saltoun with a bouquet before the naming ceremony of Laura Moncur, 26 August 1961. (By courtesy of John Innes).

▼ On board Laura Moncur for her naming ceremony are, left to right, Bowman John Innes, Alex Slater, Coxswain William Stewart, James Roy, Mechanic Jack Cole, James Murray and John Murray. (By courtesy of John Innes)

Many of the services undertaken by Laura Moncur involved helping local fishing vessels, and late on the afternoon of 16 November 1964 she went to the seine-netter Heathery Brae, which was in difficulties eight miles north-east of Buckie in very rough seas and a north-westerly gale. By the time the lifeboatmen reached the casualty, she had been taken in tow by another fishing vessel and so the lifeboat escorted them both back to harbour.

In the early hours of 9 June 1965 she went to another seine net fishing boat, Mistletoe, which had gone aground in dense fog on the west side of Buckpool Harbour. With visibility just ten yards in places, the lifeboatmen could only slowly go about searching for the stranded boat. Once the vessel had been found, the lifeboatmen attached a tow line and, on the high tide, the boat was pulled clear and escorted into the harbour by the lifeboat.

On 10 October 1967 Laura Moncur was involved in a fine rescue. She put to sea at 1.35am after the fishing vessel Briar Rose, which had a crew of eight, went aground on the West Muck Rocks in a strong northerly wind and choppy seas. Once on scene, the lifeboat crew used their searchlight to assess the casualty's situation, and it was seen that the vessel had a forty-five degree list to port and was rolling and pounding heavily in the westerly swell. Four other fishing boats were standing by, but none was able to come close enough to offer assistance.

At this point the skipper shouted that his boat was breaking up, so instead of anchoring the lifeboat and veering down towards the fishing boat as he originally intended, Coxswain George Jappy took the lifeboat straight towards the casualty. At the first pass two men were rescued, but the lifeboat was swept away by waves washing back from the rocks. On the second run in, a nylon line was made fast to the stem of the fishing boat and a further three men were rescued before the lifeboat was again swept away. Using the rope, Coxswain Jappy was able to take the lifeboat back alongside for a third time and the last three men were taken off the fishing vessel.

The lifeboat landed the survivors in the harbour in the early hours, after a very difficult rescue. For this excellent service, the RNLI accorded Coxswain Jappy the Thanks Inscribed on Vellum, and Vellum Service Certificates went to the rest of the crew for their part in the service: Second Coxswain J. Innes, Bowman J. Murray, Motor Mechanic J. G. Cole, and crew members A. Slater, R. Davidson, W. Jappy and G. Smith.

Just over four months after this rescue, another excellent service was carried out by the Buckie lifeboat crew. In the early hours of 21 February 1968 the fishing boat Mistletoe went aground at the mouth of the river Spey, so the reserve lifeboat George and Sarah Strachan, a 45ft 6in Watson on temporary duty, immediately put out. At 1.35am she reached the vessel and found it rolling heavily and being pounded by a heavy, confused swell only 350 yards from the beach.

Three other fishing vessels, Arcturus, Lead Us and Orion, were standing by, and the skipper of Arcturus asked Coxswain Jappy to transfer a towline from Mistletoe. However, getting the lifeboat close to the casualty was difficult in the broken water, so a rocket line was fired across which was used to secure

◀ Coxswain George Jappy served in the post from 1962 to 1972.

▼ Laura Moncur at moorings in No.3 Basin, with the sheds of Buckie Shipyard in the background. In autumn 1970 she was fitted with radar during a refit. (By courtesy of the RNLI)

▶ Crew of Laura Moncur in the 1970s, from left to right, Second Coxswain G. Wood, Second Mechanic James Roy, Bowman R. Davidson, Mechanic Jack Cole, crew members G. Phillip and A. Geddes Wood, and Coxswain Captain Tom Garden. Captain Garden took over as Coxswain in August 1972 and served until October 1974, when George Wood was appointed to the post. Captain Garden was also Harbour Master and, from 1973, served as the station's Honorary Secretary. (By courtesy of Buckie RNLI)

a rope. This was taken to Arcturus, 450 yards out to sea, by the lifeboat crew. But with the deck of the lifeboat coated in ice, the towline froze solid and, although it was secured aboard Arcturus, when the fishing vessel took up the strain the rope parted. The skipper of Arcturus then supplied a nylon towline, which was passed to Mistletoe by the lifeboatmen, but this line also parted when the weight was taken. Mistletoe was now rolling and pounding heavily, with waves breaking across her deck. At 4.12am her skipper informed Coxswain Jappy that he was concerned for the safety of his crew with conditions becoming too dangerous to stay on board.

Coxswain Jappy then took the lifeboat alongside the casualty, having signalled to her crew to be ready to jump. Parachute flares were fired by the coastguard from the shore to illuminate the scene, and with the help of these and the lifeboat's searchlight the lifeboat was brought alongside Mistletoe's port side, enabling the crew of six to jump onto the lifeboat, helped by the lifeboat crew. Rum and hot food were given to the survivors and the lifeboat reached Buckie at 4.50am, when the survivors were landed.

▶ The reserve 45ft 6in Watson motor lifeboat W. and S. on duty at Buckie in the late 1960s. She was on station from September 1968 to April 1969, undertaking a single service launch.

For his outstanding seamanship, skill and courage Coxswain Jappy was awarded the RNLI the Bronze medal, with Medal Service Certificates going to the other members of the crew: Second Coxswain James Murray, Motor Mechanic John G. Cole, Assistant Motor Mechanic James G. Roy, Crew Members Alexander Slater,

◀ Laura Moncur moored at her East Basin berth in about 1965, with her superstructure painted grey. (By courtesy of John Innes)

Roderick Davidson, James Coull, Robert Garden, and Alex Cursiter, District Engineer Scotland, who was visiting the station at the time. A framed Letter of Thanks signed by the Chairman of the Institution, Admiral Sir Wilfred Woods, KCB, DSO, was sent to the skipper of Arcturus.

Laura Moncur returned to station later in 1968, and undertook a couple more services, one in December 1968 and another in August 1969, before the reserve 51ft Barnett Southern Africa, built for Dover in 1949, came to the station for a short stint and Laura Moncur again left. While at Buckie, on 23 March 1970, Southern Africa launched to the fishing vessel Regal, with a crew of two, which was drifting towards the rocks, a quarter of a mile from Buckie Harbour. By the time the lifeboat arrived the

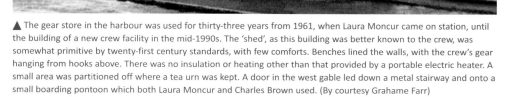

▲ The gear store in the harbour was used for thirty-three years from 1961, when Laura Moncur came on station, until the building of a new crew facility in the mid-1990s. The 'shed', as this building was better known to the crew, was somewhat primitive by twenty-first century standards, with few comforts. Benches lined the walls, with the crew's gear hanging from hooks above. There was no insulation or heating other than that provided by a portable electric heater. A small area was partitioned off where a tea urn was kept. A door in the west gable led down a metal stairway and onto a small boarding pontoon which both Laura Moncur and Charles Brown used. (By courtesy Grahame Farr)

► Laura Moncur at moorings after she had been modified to be fully self-righting. She was one of five 47ft Watson lifeboats to be so converted. (By courtesy of the RNLI)

vessel was already on the rocks, so a tow-line was secured, and the lifeboat pulled the boat clear and towed her to harbour.

Back on station during summer 1970, Laura Moncur saved the fishing boat Ray of Hope on 29 September, before performing three services the following year. After going to the yacht La Perouse on 14 June 1971, on 8 August she was called out to search for the 20ft motor yacht Lillian, with one man on board, which had been reported overdue while on passage from Findochty to Hopeman. The boat was eventually found near the West Mucks, with engine failure, so the lifeboat towed her to Buckie. The last service of the year took place in the early hours of 9 December 1971 after the coaster Barbara J came ashore in Burghead Bay in rough seas and a westerly gale. As the six crew on the coaster were in no immediate danger, the lifeboat put into Burghead Harbour and waited there until just after 9am, by when the coaster required no further assistance.

In March 1972 another relief lifeboat, the 47ft Watson Pentland (Civil Service No.32), formerly at Thurso, arrived at Buckie so that Laura Moncur could go to William Osborne's yard at Littlehampton, where she was converted into a self-righter. Following the capsize of non-self-righting lifeboats from Longhope in 1969 and Fraserburgh in 1970, the RNLI realised that making lifeboats self-righting was a priority. Many of the larger Watson and Barnett class boats were fitted with an air-bag, which inflated automatically in the event of a capsize. Some 47ft Watsons were converted to become inherently self-righting by having the engine-room compartment extended and the aft-cabin modified, thus creating a larger superstructure. Laura Moncur was one of five Watsons to which these major alterations were made.

While at Buckie, Pentland did not undertake any effective services and Laura Moncur returned in 1975 to resume her duties, having been altered notably externally. She was called out on the morning of 30 October 1976 after the tug Monarch Service, which was at anchor in the Moray Firth six miles from Buckie, requested assistance. One of her crew had been injured and the lifeboat was called on to bring the man ashore. The injured man and an interpreter were brought off by the lifeboat and landed at Buckie. The injured man went first to Buckie Hospital and then Elgin Hospital for x-rays, after which the lifeboat took the two men back to their ship.

In rapidly deteriorating conditions on the evening of 1 November 1976 the motor boat Barbara Ann, of Lossiemouth, was reported overdue. Two people were on board having been on a fishing trip about eight miles north-east of Hopeman. Laura Moncur put out at 10pm and, in rough seas and a near gale-force south-easterly wind, her crew began to search for the missing boat. By 2.30am nothing had been found, so the search was called off until first light, although the lifeboat remained at sea throughout the night. At 8.20am the missing boat was spotted by the crew of a Nimrod aircraft and the position was then radioed to the lifeboatmen. The lifeboat reached the casualty at 8.45am and saved the two men on board. The boat was towed to Burghead harbour, after which the lifeboat returned to station, reaching Buckie at 1.30pm having spent more than fifteen hours at sea.

While Laura Moncur was away in 1978 undergoing a routine overhaul, the relief lifeboat Ramsay-Dyce, a 52ft Barnett class boat, originally stationed at Aberdeen, was sent to Buckie and served at the station from March to August during which time she carried out just one service. She launched at 8.15pm on 13 April to the local fishing vessel Glen Rinnes, which was on fire off Burghead. In poor visibility the lifeboat proceeded at full speed to the scene and reached the casualty just over an hour after putting out. By that time, the boat's three crew had managed to contain the fire, but the boat was proving difficult to manoeuvre. The lifeboat therefore escorted the crippled boat slowly towards Buckie, and both vessels arrived there at 10.45pm.

Laura Moncur returned from survey on 7 August 1978 and resumed service, launching just four days later to the motor boat Star Taurus. Her next service came almost two years later, on 24 July 1980, after

▼ Laura Moncur landing the bodies of the Fraserburgh lifeboat crew in January 1970. The Fraserburgh lifeboat Duchess of Kent capsized on service to the Danish fishing vessel Opal with the loss of five crew. (By courtesy of the RNLI)

▶ Laura Moncur leaving harbour towards the end of her career at Buckie. (By courtesy of Buckie RNLI)

▼ 47ft Watson motor Laura Moncur pictured after she had been converted into a self-righter. (By courtesy of Buckie RNLI)

one of the lifeboatmen saw red flares being fired from a small fishing vessel just over a mile west of Buckie. Laura Moncur put to sea just after 7pm and found the casualty, which had two crew on board. The boat's propeller had been lost, so the lifeboat towed her to harbour and returned to her station at 7.45pm after a routine service.

During 1982 Laura Moncur completed three effective service. The first was on 9 May 1982 after a small motor boat with three people on board broke down four miles north-east of Buckie. As soon as details of the casualty had been received at 10.25pm, Laura Moncur left harbour at full speed. The

people on board the disabled boat fired a red flare which was seen by the lifeboatmen, who fired a white parachute flare in response. The lifeboat reached the casualty at 10.55pm and saved the three people, while taking their boat in tow back to Buckie. The lifeboat also went out on service on 30 May to the broken down motor boat Blue Dawn, and the other service of the year took place on 19 August when she stood by the fishing vessel Fram.

The last services by Laura Moncur were performed during 1983. On the afternoon of 27 January the fishing vessel Robert Scott was reported missing. As soon as this information had been received at the lifeboat station, the maroons were fired and Laura Moncur put to sea at 2.55pm, heading out into rough seas and a very strong north-westerly wind. The lifeboat headed towards the last known position of the fishing vessel. At 3.30pm the missing vessel was sighted by another boat and Coxswain McDonald altered course to intercept her, reaching Robert Scott fifteen minutes later. The lifeboat escorted the vessel to Buckie and returned to her moorings at 5pm.

Another routine service on 18 July 1983 proved to be the last undertaken by Laura Moncur while at Buckie. At 9.25am she went to the aid of the salmon coble Melrose II, with five crew on board. The vessel was disabled after its engine had failed two miles west of Buckie. The disabled boat was towed back to harbour, with the two vessels arriving there just over an hour after the lifeboat had first launched.

On 18 August 1983 Laura Moncur was taken to Herd & Mackenzie's boatyard for overhaul, and, although it was planned she would return, she never served at Buckie again. The relief lifeboat Royal British Legion Jubilee, a 48ft 6in Solent self-righter, was placed on temporary duty at the station, and she answered one call during her eight months of service. This was on 1 September 1983, when she was called out at 10.32am to search to the east of Buckie for an overdue pleasure craft. The search was called off by the coastguard at 11.30am and the lifeboat returned to Buckie at noon.

◀ After service at Buckie, Laura Moncur was placed in the Relief Fleet for four years, serving at Appledore amongst other stations. She was sold out of service in November 1988 and became a pleasure boat on the south coast, renamed Chizz. Following a change of ownership, she was moved to Lowestoft Haven Marina, where she is pictured in September 2009. (Nicholas Leach)

Charles Brown

▶ 52ft Arun Charles Brown on trials shortly after being built. (By courtesy of the RNLI)

When Laura Moncur reached the end of her service life, a 52ft Arun class self-righter was allocated to the station to replace her. The Arun class had been developed during the 1970s as a fast lifeboat to replace the Barnett and Watson lifeboats at stations where the boat was kept afloat. The Arun was an ideal lifeboat for Buckie, as a suitable berth was readily available in the harbour.

Work on building the new Arun began at Halmatic Ltd, at Havant, in June 1982, and in October 1982 the hull was taken to William Osborne's yard at Littlehampton to be fitted out. She was fitted with twin 485hp Caterpillar 3208TA diesel engines, which gave her a top speed of eighteen knots. She was completed during 1983 and in February 1984 taken to the RNLI Depot at Poole for final trials.

The new lifeboat, which cost £383,638.56, had been funded by David Robinson, who had previously given the money to provide a new lifeboat for Penlee. She was named Charles Brown in memory of a close friend and colleague of the donor. Crew training took place at Poole during March 1994, and she then sailed for Buckie.

The passage from Poole saw the boat call at Newlyn to visit her sister boat at Penlee, Mabel Alice, and then she headed north for Holyhead on Anglesey, crossed to Port St Mary on the Isle of Man, before making for Oban, which was the

Charles Brown

On station	5 April 1984 – May 2003
Record	270 launches, 172 lives saved
Official Number	1093 (operational no.52-27)
Donor	Gift of Mr David Robinson
Cost	£383,638.56
Dimensions	52ft x 17ft
Type	Arun
Builder	1984, hull by Halmatic Ltd, Havant; fitted out William Osborne, Littlehampton, yard no.WO 2650
Disposal	Served in Relief Fleet 2003-04, sold November 2005 to China Rescue & Salvage Bureau

◀ Charles Brown arriving
at Buckie for the first
time on 5 April 1984,
escorted by relief 48ft 6in
Solent Royal British Legion
Jubilee. (By courtesy of
Buckie RNLI)

last overnight stop before the final leg of her journey. From Oban she was
taken through the Caledonian Canal and out of the river Ness, heading east
to Buckie. She was escorted home by the relief 48ft 6in Solent Royal British
Legion Jubilee, and on 5 April 1984 was placed on service.

Charles Brown was formally named at a ceremony at Buckie harbour on
25 August 1984 by Mrs Constance Brown, by which time she had already
undertaken four services. The Duke of Atholl, chairman of the RNLI, delivered
the lifeboat to the station and Captain T. Garden, honorary secretary,
accepted her. The service of dedication was conducted by the Rev J. R.
Osbeck, assisted by the Rev A. Barr and the Rev T. N. Johnston, after which
Mrs Brown, escorted by the Divisional Inspector for Scotland North, John
Unwin, moved to the dais and christened the lifeboat. As the champagne
bottle broke over the lifeboat's bow, an air-sea rescue helicopter flew past
flying the RNLI house flag from its winch wire.

Charles Brown served at Buckie for almost twenty years, during which
time she gained a fine record of service, launching 270 times on service

◀ Charles Brown on
the day she arrived at
Buckie, 5 April 1984, is
put through her paces in
Cullen Bay. (By courtesy
of Buckie RNLI)

▶ Charles Brown is greeted by a crowd of supporters and well-wishers as she arrives at Buckie for the first time, 5 April 1984. (By courtesy of Buckie RNLI)

and saving more than 170 lives. Her first rescues had been undertaken before her naming ceremony, and just eleven days before the christening she answered two calls in the space of seven hours. On 14 August 1984 she launched at 10.20am to the fishing boat North Star, which had broken down near the East Muck Rocks with a crew of one. The boat was towed back to the harbour and the lifeboat returned to her moorings, only to be called out again five hours later to another small fishing boat, Dawn Wind. The vessel was in trouble a mile and a half west of the harbour with a fouled propeller, so Charles Brown towed it back to harbour in a routine operation.

As Charles Brown was on passage from Lossiemouth to Buckie on 6 July 1985, reports were received that a yacht had gone aground at Findochty. The lifeboat immediately went to assist and found the yacht Seon-Na-Mara, with eight people on board, in difficulty. The crew of the motor boat Julie had managed to get a line aboard the yacht, so the lifeboat's inflatable Y boat was launched to stand by while the yacht was pulled free. The casualty was then towed into Findochty Harbour, the Y boat was recovered and the lifeboat returned to station.

▼ Some of the crew who undertook the passage bringing Charles Brown from Poole to her station: left to right, Chris Wild, Geddes Wood, Kenny Farquhar and Coxswain Willie McDonald. (By courtesy of Buckie RNLI)

Between September 1985 and May 1986 the relief lifeboat A. J. R. and L. G. Uridge was on temporary duty while Charles Brown went to Jones Boatyard for overhaul. The relief boat was called out three times during her stint at Buckie. The first time, on 2 December 1985, saw her searching for a missing cabin cruiser, Tern, and its single crewman. The lifeboat searched until, at 8.10pm, a light was seen. The lifeboat went to investigate and found the boat, which was towed back to Buckie.

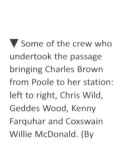

A few days after Charles Brown returned from overhaul in May 1986, she helped a sick woman on board the fishing vessel Shona II. Of the other services undertaken that year, two were to the same craft, the fishing boat Hustler. On the afternoon of 24 June 1986 the fishing boat broke down eight miles east of Buckie. Charles Brown reached the casualty within half an hour of launching and took three men aboard while the disabled boat was towed to Cullen Harbour. On 4 November Hustler broke down 400 yards off Logie Head and Charles Brown again towed the vessel to Cullen Harbour.

On 17-18 July 1987 Charles Brown and her crew were involved in two fine services. In force six to seven south-easterly winds and rough seas, the lifeboat first launched to the auxiliary yacht Samphire, which had damaged sails about twenty miles north of Macduff. With the lifeboat having to contend with strong winds, gusting above forty knots and creating a heavy swell, Coxswain John Murray reduced speed to ten knots as he approached the search area. The yacht was picked up by radar, with the lifeboat reaching the casualty at 9.20pm to first establish that the three occupants were safe. The yacht's engine was then started, the sails were stowed and Charles Brown escorted her to Macduff Harbour, where the boats arrived at 10pm.

The lifeboat returned to station at 11.30pm, but two hours later launched again, this time to the 50ft Swedish topsail schooner Monsoon, of Ekero, which had broken down five miles north-east of Portknockie. The strong winds and heavy swell continued to make it difficult for the lifeboatmen, but on clearing the harbour Coxswain Murray set course at full speed for the casualty's reported position. Monsoon was eventually found seven miles

▼ Charles Brown at moorings in the harbour, August 1994. (Nicholas Leach)

north-west of Burghead, with her anchor down. Her engine was unusable and she was pitching heavily in the rough seas and heavy swell. At 3.16am, as Charles Brown approached the yacht, her anchor line was cut free.

The vessel's four occupants were not injured and did not want to transfer to the lifeboat, so a towline was passed across and secured, and the tow taken up at dead slow speed. The sheering of the yacht in the heavy weather made progress slow, with the wind now force eight. As land was approached, the towline was shortened, and Charles Brown and the yacht approached Burghead from the south-west. Near the harbour entrance the swell caused the lifeboat and her tow to sheer violently, but the entrance was negotiated safely and the yacht was secured alongside at 5.49am. Charles Brown left Burghead at 6.15pm and arrived back at Buckie at 7.25pm.

In recognition of the dedication displayed by Coxswain Murray and his crew during these two difficult services, a framed Letter of Thanks signed by the Duke of Atholl, Chairman of the RNLI, was presented to Coxswain Murray, Acting Second Coxswain Kenneth Farquhar, Mechanic George Stewart, and crew members Phillip Latchem, Gordon Lawtie and Steven Matheson.

In February 1990 Charles Brown was involved in a long service to the fishing vessel Emma Thomson II, which had run aground at the West Mucks with six people on board. The lifeboat went out three times to the vessel, which was in danger of sinking. She first put to sea at 8.41pm on 20 February and, on reaching the scene, the lifeboatmen found the local pilot boat alongside. The lifeboat made an unsuccessful attempt to tow the fishing vessel clear and then two lifeboatmen went aboard with a portable pump.

Another unsuccessful attempt was made to pull the vessel clear, but the casualty's situation began to deteriorate rapidly, beginning to list to starboard while being pounded heavily. Coxswain Murray decided the vessel had to be evacuated so the lifeboat's inflatable Y boat was launched at 9.30pm and

▼ Charles Brown on service to the fishing boat Hebridean on 16 May 1996. (Nicholas Leach)

used to take off the two lifeboatmen. The pilot boat took off the fishing vessel's crew and the portable pumps while another fishing vessel arrived on scene with more pumps so, at 10.10pm, the lifeboat returned to station.

She put out again to the fishing vessel at 12.15am, on 21 February, taking two extra lifeboat crew as well as surveyors from the casualty's insurance company. Using the Y boat, three lifeboatmen boarded the stranded vessel, taking with them another pump, and one of the surveyors also went aboard. With the water level in the casualty falling, they all returned to the lifeboat, which made for Buckie. The lifeboat went out again at 7.20am to put some of the fishermen back on their boat, while a tow line from the fishing vessel Blue Angel was secured to the stranded vessel. The casualty was then slowly pulled clear of the rocks and the engines restarted. Although water was flooding the damaged vessel, she entered Buckie Harbour under her own power, escorted by the lifeboat, and was beached at the North Pier.

Another challenging service was carried out on 17 August 1991 after a mayday message was sent out by the fishing vessel Fidelity, which had gone aground. Just after 3am Charles Brown, with Coxswain John Murray at the helm, was heading towards the casualty at full speed in westerly force three winds. Using the searchlight, the lifeboat crew spotted the fishing vessel hard aground with her starboard rail under water. The survivors were assumed to be in the life raft and drifting ashore. However, as the searchlight was retrained on the fishing vessel, a flashing torch on the port side of the casualty signalled the presence of three survivors. The life raft was only partially inflated, and lying unused off the port quarter.

With the fishing vessel listing about forty degrees to starboard and the swell preventing use of the inflatable Y boat due to a risk of capsize, Coxswain Murray went straight to the fishing vessel, which was on the north side of a reef in very shallow water. With the starboard engine in neutral in case of damage to the propeller, the lifeboat approached the casualty as slowly as possible. Coxswain Murray succeeded in putting the bow of the lifeboat close to the survivors, and at 3.13am the lifeboat crew helped them scramble onto the bow of the lifeboat, which then went gently astern on the port engine to clear the casualty and the reef. The lifeboat touched bottom three times at her stern before she was clear, but was then able to return to Buckie harbour, and land the three survivors.

Divisional inspector for Scotland North, Les Vipond, noted in his report that, 'It took only twenty-seven minutes from the time of the first alert to landing the three survivors. Coxswain John Murray, aware that the survivors were in great danger, chose to approach the casualty without delay while accepting that his lifeboat could suffer some damage. He showed very good seamanship in accomplishing the task on one engine only.' Coxswain Murray was congratulated on his 'leadership, determination and skill' during the service in a letter from the RNLI's Chairman, Michael Vernon.

Later on 17 August, with the lifeboat back at her moorings, the small Y class inflatable was launched from the Arun and went back to Fidelity to assess the damage. As the Y boat was being recovered, a young woman jumped into the harbour in an apparent suicide attempt. While the Y boat was being launched again, lifeboatman Steven Matheson was driven round the harbour by his wife and jumped into the water to help. He managed to get a life belt, which had been thrown into the water by a passer-by, over the woman's shoulders and pulled her to the stern of one of the fishing vessels.

▼ Charles Brown on exercise in rough seas. (By courtesy of the RNLI)

At this point the Y boat arrived on scene, took both the woman and Matheson from the water, and landed them at the lifeboat station. For his gallantry, and disregard for his own safety in entering the water to help the

◀ Dramatic photographs of Charles Brown on exercise in rough seas off Buckie harbour. (By courtesy of the RNLI)

woman, Matheson was awarded the Royal Humane Society's Testimonial on Parchment, as well as a letter of congratulations from the RNLI's Chief of Operations, Commodore George Cooper, who said 'Your quick response and actions saved this woman's life and brought great credit to the Institution'.

Towards the end of 1992, on 12 November, Charles Brown was called out in gale force conditions. She launched at 10.37pm and headed out into very rough seas and a north-westerly gale to the 22ft yacht Hobo, which had been reported in difficulties. The yacht was found ten miles east of Buckie with its sole occupant struggling to keep his vessel's head to sea with an outboard engine. A tow line was secured through the bow fairlead and to the foot of the mast, but five minutes after the tow began Coxswain Murray decided it was too dangerous to leave the man on the yacht so it was hauled alongside and the man was transferred to the lifeboat. The tow then got under way again and the vessels reached Buckie at 1.30am on 13 November.

◄ Charles Brown on exercise off the harbour with Coxswain John Murray on the flying bridge. (Nicholas Leach)

At the harbour entrance, Coxswain Murray slowed the lifeboat down to allow the 100ft beam trawler Blue Angel to enter harbour first, but just as the trawler came to the entrance she was struck by an exceptionally large wave, which pushed her off course and she rammed the West Pier. The next wave swung the vessel round broadside and jammed her between the North and West Piers, blocking the harbour entrance. Coxswain Murray swung the lifeboat round into the wind and headed towards the West Mucks Reef, intending to anchor the yacht there and go to the assistance of the trawler. But the crew of the trawler secured a line from the vessel's stern onto the North Pier and the trawler was pulled round, using the winch, until her bows were back in the channel again and she was able to enter harbour safely.

The lifeboat headed back towards the harbour but, just thirty yards from the entrance, the bow fairlead on the yacht broke and, with the tow line pulling directly on the mast, the yacht was swung broadside on. Coxswain Murray had to use his skill with the lifeboat's engines and rudders to counteract the rapid runs of the yacht. At one point, the yacht struck the port quarter of the lifeboat, but the vessels entered harbour at 1.50am.

During the 1990s the relief Arun lifeboat Edith Emilie was on station a number of times while Charles Brown went for refit. She was on duty from July to November 1990, August to September 1991, November 1992 to February 1993, and April to July 1995. During the last of these periods she was called out during the afternoon of 25 June 1995 to help three swimmers who had got into difficulties off Sunnyside Beach. However, they managed to get ashore safely and were taken to hospital by ambulance, suffering only from cold, so the lifeboat returned to her moorings.

Just over an hour later Edith Emilie was called out again to help the 36ft yacht Vanagis, with two crew, which had gone ashore close to Covesea lighthouse. On reaching the scene at 8.20pm, Coxswain Murray found the yacht on the beach so the lifeboat's Y boat was launched. Meanwhile, Coxswain Murray tried to find the best way to manoeuvre the lifeboat as close as possible to the casualty and, once the lifeboat was as close as she could get, the Y boat's crew carried a long tow line to the yacht so that the lifeboat could pull it off. But the yacht was firmly aground and was not pulled clear until 9.10pm. The yacht's crew managed to start the auxiliary engine and, escorted by the lifeboat, made for Lossiemouth, where they berthed forty minutes later and the lifeboat returned to station.

On 16 May 1996 Charles Brown, back on station after survey, completed a fine service. In choppy seas and a freshening wind, she went to the fishing boat Hebrides which had been pushed in amongst rocks near Findochty harbour. Within ten minutes of launching, the lifeboat was on scene and the crew found the boat just 15ft from rocks on either side. The lifeboat, which had to be kept in position by her engines, was taken to within 25ft of the casualty and a line was passed across, being secured at the first attempt. In the heavy swell, the lifeboat was carefully taken stern first out to sea, getting the casualty clear after it had struck rocks initially. The tow was transferred to the stern of the lifeboat and the casualty was taken to Findochty harbour.

On 3 July 1997 some Buckie lifeboat volunteers were involved in helping evacuate people stranded by floods in Elgin, seventeen miles to the east. The coastguard contacted Honorary Secretary John Fowlie requesting helpers as well as small boats in case residents needed to be evacuated from their homes, as water was 4ft deep in some areas. At 9pm eight crew members left Buckie with an inflatable Y boat and an inflatable Z boat, which had been

▼ Charles Brown leaving harbour on exercise. (Nicholas Leach)

taken from relief lifeboats at Buckie Shipyard. They arrived in Elgin half an hour later and stood by in one district of the city until the early hours of 4 July, at which point they were stood down as the flood level was dropping.

Charles Brown and her crew performed an unusual service on 18 July 1997 when they were asked to launch to the yacht Ovation, which had been seen going round in circles just off the harbour and whose skipper was acting in a very dangerous manner. The lifeboat put out at 11pm and went alongside the casualty ten minutes later only for the lifeboat crew to be sworn at by the drunk skipper and told they were not welcome. They therefore returned to harbour, picked up two policemen and returned to the vessel. The skipper was then arrested by the policemen, taken on board the lifeboat and three lifeboat crew went onto the yacht. The skipper and the police were landed in the harbour, after which the lifeboat returned to the yacht to tow it in.

Buckie lifeboat crew used two lifeboats to effect a service on 7 February 1998. At 7.40pm the coaster Oakland was seen to go on the rocks near Mucks Beacon, 400 metres north of the harbour entrance. Although communication with Oakland suggested that the vessel was alright, when it was realised the vessel was aground the coastguard asked the lifeboat to launch. Charles Brown put out at 8.06pm and two minutes later was followed by the relief lifeboat Edith Emilie, which was lying at the station and the use of which was authorised by RNLI Headquarters at Poole as an extra boat, given the size and position of the casualty, as she could provide useful assistance. It was thought that two boats might be able to tow the casualty off.

▼ In 1994 work started on a new crew room and shore facility on Commercial Road on the same site as the existing shed, the facilities in which were out-dated. The new building was completed in spring 1995 and provided the volunteer crew with greatly improved training and changing facilities. The new building was formally opened on 26 August 1995 by The Hon Mrs Henry Douglas-Home, a Vice-Convenor of the Scottish Lifeboat Council. (Nicholas Leach)

◀ 52ft Arun Charles Brown at the newly-created berth next to the shore facility in 1998. She gave nineteen years of service to Buckie during which time she saved 172 lives. (Nicholas Leach)

The fishing vessel Aurora, which was in the vicinity, offered to help. For the next hour four attempts were made to tow Oakland off the rocks, using the combined efforts of the two lifeboats and the fishing vessel. The tow from the fishing vessel parted twice, and the lifeboats were no more successful. At 9.35pm Charles Brown took four crewmen ashore leaving the captain, first officer and engineer on board, while Edith Emilie stood by as the tide dropped. Charles Brown took over at 11.15pm and stood by until 2.30am on 8 February, by which time the vessel was no longer in danger of capsizing.

On 11 August 2000 a small fishing boat was saved just in time after she got into difficulties close to rocks off Buckie. The lifeboat crew were out in the harbour completing engine trials on the relief Arun Duchess of Kent, and as soon as the coastguard informed them that a small boat had fouled her propellers close to Scarnose Point the lifeboat was on her way. The casualty asked over the radio when the lifeboat would arrive, to which coastguards advised 'About five minutes', with the reply 'That may be in time'. Five minutes later, the lifeboat reached the scene to find the casualty just 6ft from the rocks. A tow line was quickly passed, the vessel was pulled clear, and then towed into Portknockie, arriving twenty-five minutes later.

The last service by the 52ft Arun Charles Brown took place on 20 February 2003, and proved to be another routine tow. She launched at 8.30pm to the fishing boat Loyal Friend, which had engine problems a mile north of Portsoy. The lifeboat reached the casualty just after 9pm, rigged a tow and at 10.38pm entered Buckie harbour with the casualty in tow.

Replaced at Buckie in May 2003 having served the station for nineteen years, Charles Brown served as a relief lifeboat for a further year before being put up for sale. She was bought by the China Rescue & Salvage Bureau in late 2005, one of several Aruns bought for service in China. She was shipped to China via Felixstowe on a container ship in December 2005 and, after being renamed Huaying 396, became one of three boats stationed at Yan Tai.

William Blannin

◀ William Blannin is turned upside down at DML Dockyard, Devonport, Plymouth, for self-righting trials. She righted herself within sex seconds. (Supplied by Buckie RNLI)

I n May 2003 a new 17m Severn class lifeboat arrived at Buckie. The lifeboat was one of a new generation of faster all-weather lifeboats being introduced by the RNLI. In the 1990s two new designs had been developed, the 17m Severn and 14m Trent, which were capable of twenty-five knots at full speed and incorporated the latest equipment and technology to make rescue work safer, easier and more efficient.

The larger of the two types, the Severn, was deemed ideal for rescue work off Buckie and, in July 2002, the RNLI announced that a new Severn, due to be completed in February 2003, had been allocated to the station. The new lifeboat, self-righting by virtue of the inherent buoyancy in the watertight wheelhouse, was moulded in fibre reinforced composite at Green Marine's Lymington boatyard and the hull was fitted out by DML at Devonport, Plymouth. Twin Caterpillar 3412 diesel engines, each of 1,250bhp, provided the power, and the boat was fitted with the latest navigational aids.

In announcing the decision to allocate a Severn to Buckie, RNLI operations director Michael Vlasto said: 'Buckie station is situated thirty-nine miles from Invergordon, sixty miles from Wick, sixteen miles from Macduff and thirty-two miles from Fraserburgh. It provides all-weather lifeboat cover from Burghead to Macduff and out to the Beatrice Oil Field and the Smith Bank. In October 1997 the RNLI coast review delegation visited

William Blannin	
On station	27 May 2003 –
Official Number	1268 (operational no.17-37)
Donor	Legacies of Kenneth Maurice Williams, of Salisbury, and Jean M. Lamont, together with other legacies and gifts
Cost	£1,900,000
Dimensions	17.28m x 5.5m x 3.3m
Type	Severn
Builder	2003, hull by Green Marine, Lymington; fitted out by DML, Plymouth; yard no.054

◄ Lifeboat crew on board William Blannin at the RNLI Depot, Poole, during crew training. The are, left to right, John C. Murray (Coxswain), Gordon Lawtie (Mechanic), and crew members Steven Smith, Kevin Herd, Kevin McKay and David Grant. (By courtesy of Buckie RNLI)

Buckie following which it was agreed that a Severn class all-weather lifeboat would be allocated to replace the current Arun class.'

After crew training had taken place towards the end of April 2003, the new Severn left the RNLI Depot at Poole on 3 May and set out on passage up the west coast of England and Wales, and north to her new station. She called first at Newlyn then crossed the Irish Sea to Rosslare Harbour, before heading to Port St Mary and Oban, where the crew was changed for the final leg of the journey home. She stopped at Corpach on 7 May, and went through the Caledonian Canal to Inverness on 8 May. After staying overnight in Inverness, the new Severn was brought to Buckie. The boat was manned by Coxswain John Charles Murray, Mechanic Gordon Lawtie, Kevin Herd, David Grant, and Steven Smith, who were accompanied by Divisional Inspector John Davies and Deputy Divisional Engineer Tom Peebles.

◄ William Blannin (on right) moored alongside the pontoon with 52ft Arun Charles Brown on 9 May 2003. (Bob Williams)

The new lifeboat arrived at Buckie on 9 May 2003 and was escorted into the harbour by Charles Brown. Coxswain John Murray was then presented with a long service badge for twenty-two years of service, while Golden Jubilee Medals were given to a number of the crew. After a week at Buckie, the new boat was taken south and represented the RNLI at the International Festival of the Sea at Leith, held during the late May Bank Holiday from 22 to 26 May 2003. During the event, she was open to the public and an estimated 5,000 people took the opportunity to go aboard. She returned from Leith on 27 May 2003 and the following day was officially placed on station.

The new boat was named William Blannin after the man whose bequest had provided the principal funding for the lifeboat, Kenneth Maurice Williams, of Salisbury, who died in May 1998. The name was a combination of the deceased's name and the maiden name of the late Mrs Williams. A number of other legacies and gifts made up the funding for the new boat, which had cost approximately £1.9 million to build.

William Blannin was formally named and dedicated on 2 August 2003 at a ceremony overseen by Alex Fowler, chairman of the branch. The boat was handed over by Derwent Campbell, executor of the estate of the late Kenneth Williams, and was accepted by Andrew Cubie on behalf of the RNLI Council. The boat was accepted by Honorary Secretary John Fowlie. After a service of dedication, led by Captain Elizabeth Pritchard, Mrs Lizzie Campbell officially named the lifeboat. A presentation was then made to Mrs Campbell by Eilidh and Callum Murray, grandchildren of Coxswain and Mrs John Murray. A good crowd of supporters and well-wishers was on hand to witness the

▼ William Blannin blasts her way out of harbour. (By courtesy of the RNLI)

◄ The scene in Buckie harbour during the naming of William Blannin. During the evening after the ceremony a celebration dance was held in the Royal British Legion Club in Buckie for the guests that had attended the naming as well as family members and friends of the crew. At 8.15pm the coastguard requested that the lifeboat be launched to a yacht with two people on board, which was in trouble off Lossiemouth having lost power in difficult conditions. So the crew, in their white shirts and kilts, proceeded to the station to help the yacht. The lifeboat arrived on scene at 8.55pm and towed the yacht to the safety of Lossiemouth Harbour, returning to station at 9.50pm. The crew then returned to the celebration dance, still in their kilts and looking every bit as smart as when they left. (Nicholas Leach)

◄ After her naming ceremony, William Blannin putting out, passing the station's former lifeboat Charles Brown, then part of the RNLI's Relief Fleet, moored in the harbour. (Nicholas Leach)

▶ 17m Severn William Blannin leaving harbour on exercise in August 2009. (Nicholas Leach)

▶ William Blannin on exercise with Coxswain Alan S. Robertson on the flying bridge. (Nicholas Leach)

boat's naming, after which she put to sea with Coxswain Murray at the helm for a trip with the invited guests. Alongside the pier in the harbour was the station's former lifeboat, Charles Brown, while the relief 17m Severn Fraser Flyer (Civil Service No.43) was occupying the station's mooring berth.

Since being at Buckie, the Severn lifeboat has answered many calls. The descriptions below give a flavour of the kind of work she has carried out. Her first service came on 18 June 2003 after red flares were seen to the north of the harbour, but the lifeboat crew established that the flares had been dropped by military aircraft on exercise so the lifeboat returned to station.

During 2004 William Blannin went to the aid of several small fishing boats. On 12 May she helped the 19th creel boat Maridon, which had engine failure. The boat was drifting and in danger of foundering, so the lifeboat towed it to Portknockie. On 30 June William Blannin launched to another small fishing boat, which was sinking off Hopeman harbour. Its two occupants were airlifted to safety by Rescue helicopter 137, leaving the lifeboat to tow the vessel to the harbour. And on 5 September the fishing vessel Castlebay went ashore after her propeller had become fouled so the lifeboat towed it clear.

The first call of 2005, undertaken in force seven winds and rough seas, was executed speedily and efficiently. William Blannin launched at 8.55am to help a crewman experiencing breathing difficulties on the rig stand-by vessel Viking Viper, which was too large to enter harbour. The lifeboat reached the vessel five minutes after launching, took the casualty on board and by 9.20am was back at station to transfer the man to an ambulance.

On 29 March 2006 the lifeboat launched to the motor yacht St Kilda, which had a fouled rudder and was in trouble off Findochty harbour in rough seas. The lifeboat reached the vessel within ten minutes of launching and passed a tow across. The vessel was taken into Findochty and at 2.50pm the lifeboat was back on station, exactly an hour after the crew had been paged.

During August 2006 William Blannin was called out three times in the space of three days. On 6 August she launched at 4.15pm to a fishing vessel, which had lost power, and towed the craft to Findochty harbour. The following day the lifeboat went to a 7m fishing vessel that had gone aground. In slight seas, she helped to refloat the casualty, which had one person on board, and then towed it to Cullen harbour. William Blannin was called out for the third time

▼ William Blannin entering Buckie harbour after exercise. (Nicholas Leach)

▶ The mooring berth and crew facility in Buckie harbour, with 17m Severn William Blannin on station. (Nicholas Leach)

on 8 August, when she launched at 5.20pm to a small yacht, but she was stood down as Invergordon lifeboat went to assist the casualty.

A difficult service was undertaken on 22-23 September 2009 after the fishing vessel Spring Tide got into difficulties twenty-three nautical miles north-east of Buckie. The vessel was taking on water so the lifeboat crew prepared the salvage pump while on passage to the casualty. They found the boat with one person on board, but transferring the salvage pump was impossible as the lifeboat could not get close enough due to the casualty's severe motion, so the pump was floated across. Transferring a lifeboat man was also too dangerous in the heavy swell and at one point crew member David Grant fell, badly hurting his leg. Using the salvage pump, the boat was pumped dry, and the lifeboat then escorted the casualty to Buckie.

On 15 December 2009 a fine service was performed by the Buckie lifeboatmen after the yacht Nicari got into difficulty near Covesea Skerries. The lifeboat launched at 3.20pm and made best speed to the casualty, which had lost power and so dropped anchor. But while the anchor was being readied, the casualty drifted between two rocks. Once on scene, the lifeboat crew found it difficult to approach the casualty due to the rocks, onshore wind and heavy swell. William Blannin was approximately 100m away and, as conditions ruled out use of the inflatable Y boat, a speedline was fired to the casualty. This missed, so another was fired, and this reached the yacht, whose crew used it to pull a tow rope across. In force six winds and rough seas, the lifeboat had difficulty keeping station but once the tow rope had been made fast, the lifeboat took the strain, the anchor rope was cut and the yacht was pulled clear through a gap in the rocks. The casualty was then towed to Buckie harbour, and the lifeboat returned to station at 7.45pm.

For 150 years Buckie's volunteer lifeboat crews have shown a dedication and commitment to the cause of life-saving at sea that is second to none, and the crews and lifeboats have been ready whenever needed to undertake rescue work off the Moray coast, whatever the weather.

Lifeboats

On station	Official Number	Name / Donor	Dimensions / Type	Launches/ lives saved
1860 – 1871		Miriam Gift of an anonymous lady.	30' x 7' Peake SR	3/49
1871 – 1889		James Sturm Legacy of Mr J. Sturm, Holburn, London.	33' x 8'1" Self-righter	10/29
1889 – 1908	244	James Sharpe Legacy of Mr J. Sharpe, Shoreditch.	34' x 7'6" Self-righter	8/9
1908 – 1922	581	Maria Stephenson Legacy of Miss Maria M. Langton, Chelsea.	38' x 9'4" Watson	13/13
1922 – 1949	681	K. B. M. Legacies of W. Kirkhope, C. Chetwode Bailey, and Miss C. G. C. McInroy.	40' x 11' Watson motor	62/12
1949 – 1960	857	Glencoe, Glasgow Legacy of Mrs L. Glen, Glasgow.	41' x 11'8" Watson motor	27/9
1960 – 1961	736	W. and S. Legacy of Miss E. Young and Miss W. A. Coode.	45'6" x 12'6 Watson motor	
1961 – 1984	958	Laura Moncur Legacy of Miss L. Moncur, gift from Miss J. B. Moncur and RNLI Funds.	47' x 13' Watson motor	66/39
1984–2003	1093	Charles Brown Gift of Mr David Robinson.	52' x 17' Arun	270/172
2003–	1268	William Blannin Legacies of Mr K. M. Williams, Salisbury, Jean M. Lamont, with other legacies and gifts.	17.28m x 5.5m Severn	

◄ 17m Severn William Blannin setting out on exercise in the evening sun, April 2009. (Cliff Crone)

Services

Miriam Lifeboat
1867	Dec 2	Sloop Hellens, of Alloa, saved 4
1868	Sep 29	Eight fishing boats, saved 45

James Sturm Lifeboat
1874	Aug 14	Three fishing boats, saved 17
1876	Jan 20	Schooner Claudine, of Antwerp, assisted to save
	Apr 11	Schooner Elizabeth, of Llanelli, saved 5
1881	Oct 15	Schooner Equestrian, of Banff, saved 4
1887	Aug 7	Boat from Schooner Ben Aigen with 1 survivor from a pilot boat, saved 3

James Sharpe Lifeboat
1890	Feb 27	Fishing boats, stood by
1899	Nov 3	Lugger Welcome Home, in tow of a fishing boat, stood by
1900	May 1	Lugger Mary, of Buckie, saved vessel and 9
1903	Apr 12	Schooner Maria, of Barsel, stood by
1906	Oct 26	Fishing boat Granny Cornal, of Buckie, stood by

Maria Stephenson Lifeboat
1909	Mar 16	Lugger Superb, of Portessie, saved boat and 9
	Oct 5	Fishing boat The Boy, of Findochty, saved boat & 1
1911	Apr 19	Fishing boat Joseph, of Banff, saved boat and 3
		Fishing boats, stood by

K. B. M. Lifeboat
1922	Dec 18	Steam drifter Victory, of Portgordon, stood by
1926	Nov 14	Motor boat St Blane, of Glasgow, stood by
1927	Feb 27	Steam trawler Merleton, of Granton, gave help
1937	Jan 26	Steam trawler Sangarius, of Aberdeen, landed an injured man
1941	Mar 25	British aircraft, picked up a body and some wreckage
1942	Mar 7	HM Trawler Sheldon, gave help
	12	Trawler Morning Rays, of Fraserburgh, gave help
		Steam drifter Amity, of Buckie, gave help
	June 10	Fishing boat Quest, of Cullen, gave help
	Sep 15	RAF Launch No.170, saved 9
	Oct 23	Danish fishing boat Vesterland, stood by
	Dec 29	Danish fishing boat Vesterland, stood by
1943	May 12	British aircraft, salved wreckage
1944	May 16	Local fishing boats, stood by
	29	HM Drifter Thaw, stood by and gave help
1946	Feb 8	Admiralty motor fishing vessel No.1067, stood by
	Apr 6	Danish fishing boat Bent Erik, saved 3
1948	Dec 23	Motor vessel Airmoor II, of Buckie, escorted
1949	Jan 8	Steamship Frej, of Stockholm, landed 19

Glencoe, Glasgow Lifeboat
1951	Dec 27	Fishing vessel Cloud, of Hopeman, stood by
1953	Mar 12	Aircraft, landed a body
1954	May 9	Sailing boat, saved boat and 2
1956	Jan 21	Fishing boat Briar Bank, of Buckie, escorted boat
1958	Feb 5	Steamship Orkney Trader, of Kirkwall, stood by
	18	Fishing boat Seaforth, saved 5
	26	Fishing boat Elm Grove, took out doctor
	Dec 19	Fishing boat Spinaway, escorted vessel
1959	Jan 13	Aircraft, recovered wreckage
	Mar 19	Motor launch Rosaline, saved boat and 2

H. C. J. Reserve Lifeboat
1960	Aug 31	Search for aeroplane, nothing found (no service)

W. and S. Reserve Lifeboat
1960	Oct 1	Motor vessel Radium, gave help

Laura Moncur Lifeboat
1962	Aug 18	An aircraft, rendered assistance
1964	Mar 15	Trawler Juniper, of Aberdeen, stood by
	Nov 16	Fishing boat Heathery Brae, escorted boat
1965	June 9	Fishing boat Mistletoe, gave help
	Dec 9	Shackleton aircraft, recovered wreckage
1966	May 4	Lobster boat Rose, saved boat and 1
1967	Sep 10	A fishing boat, saved boat and 1
	Oct 10	Fishing boat Briar Rose, saved 8

George and Sarah Strachan Reserve Lifeboat
1968	Feb 21	Fishing boat Mistletoe, saved 6

Laura Moncur Lifeboat
1968	Dec 14	Yacht Thistle, saved yacht and 5
1969	Aug 12	Fishing boat Harvest Moon, landed 4, saved boat

Southern Africa Reserve Lifeboat
1970	Mar 23	Fishing boat Regal, gave help

Laura Moncur Lifeboat
1970	Sep 29	Fishing boat Ray of Hope, saved boat and 1
1971	June 14	Yacht La Perouse, saved yacht and 2
	Aug 8	Motor boat Lillian, saved boat and 1
	Dec 9	Motor vessel Barbara J, stood by

Pentland (Civil Service No.32) Relief Lifeboat
[On station while Laura Moncur went to Littlehampton for cabin modifications to give her inherent SR ability. Pentland recorded no service launches at Buckie.]

Laura Moncur on passage near Wells, Norfolk
1972	Mar 19	Motor boat Sea Quest, saved boat and 4

Laura Moncur Lifeboat
1975	Mar 6	A raft, gave help
	Apr 6	Dinghy, saved dinghy
1976	Oct 30	Tug Monarch Service, landed an injured man
	Nov 1	Motor boat Barbara Ann, saved boat and 2
1977	Nov 12	Fishing boat Elo, escorted boat

Ramsay-Dyce Relief Lifeboat
1978	Apr 13	Fishing boat Glen Rinnes, escorted boat

Laura Moncur Lifeboat
1978	Aug 11	Motor boat Star Taurus, saved boat and 3
1980	July 24	Fishing boat, gave help
1981	May 23	Motor boat Star Taurus, stood by
1982	May 9	Motor boat, saved boat and 3
	30	Motor boat Blue Dawn, landed 3 and saved boat
	Aug 19	Fishing vessel Fram, stood by
1983	Jan 27	Fishing vessel Robert Scott, escorted vessel
	July 18	Salmon coble Melrose II, saved boat and 5

Charles Brown Lifeboat
1984	July 21	Powerboat, saved boat
	Aug 14	Fishing boat North Star, saved boat and 1
		Fishing vessel Dawn Wind, gave help
	Sep 12	Yacht Liv, in tow of motor boat Mary, escorted
	16	Cabin cruiser, gave help
1985	July 6	Yacht Seon-y-Mara, stood by

A. J. R. and L. G. Uridge Relief Lifeboat
	Dec 2	Cabin cruiser Tern, saved boat and 1
1986	Jan 30	Fishing vessel Crystal River, escorted vessel
	Mar 18	Naval survey motor boat Fitzroy, gave help

Charles Brown Lifeboat
	May 15	Sick woman on fishing vessel Shona II, gave help
	June 24	Fishing vessel Hustler, saved boat and 5
	Aug 30	Yacht Swan Song, saved boat and 2
	Nov 4	Fishing vessel Hustler, gave help
1987	Mar 26	Small boat Honeybee, saved boat and 4
	May 22	Fishing boat, gave help
	June 27	Yacht, saved yacht and 1
	30	Fishing boat, escorted boat
	July 4	Motor boat, escorted boat

	July 17	Auxiliary yacht Samphire, escorted yacht
	18	Schooner Monsoon of Ekero, saved boat and 4
	Sep 15	Cabin cruiser, gave help
	Oct 10	Body in sea, landed a body
	20	Fishing vessel, gave help

Newsbuoy Relief Lifeboat

1988	Aug 7	Cabin cruiser Amy Lu, gave help
	12	Fishing vessel, recovered wreckage
	Sep 16	Fishing vessel, gave help

Charles Brown Lifeboat

	Dec 22	Fishing vessel Orcadia, saved vessel and 1
1989	Apr 4	Pleasure craft, saved craft and 2
	June 17	Fishing vessel Honey Bee, gave help
	July 1	Motor vessel Joanne, saved boat and 2
	Sep 25	Fishing vessel Connie, gave help
	Oct 3	Fishing vessel Collann, gave help
	24	Fishing vessel Esperans, saved vessel
1990	Jan 14	Tug Workhorse, gave help – craft brought in
	26	Fishing boat Winner, escorted
	Feb 11	Motor boat Iris, escorted
	20	Fishing vessel Emma Thompson, saved 2
	21	Fishing vessel Emma Thompson, gave help
	Apr 29	Small boat Rochomie, craft brought in
		Small boat Lara Anne, craft brought in
	June 16	Motor boat Gill, craft brought in
	25	Yacht Klaus Strotbecker, craft brought in

Edith Emilie Relief Lifeboat

	Aug 4	Sailing dinghy, craft brought in

Charles Brown Lifeboat

	Oct 14	Powered boat, escorted
1991	Feb 26	Yacht Homer, saved craft and 2
	May 6	Fishing boat Scorpio, escorted craft
	June 25	Pleasure boat Balmoral, craft brought in
	July 27	Cabin cruiser Skua, gave help
	Aug 17	Fishing vessel Fidelity, saved 3
	Oct 26	Canoe, saved craft
	Nov 22	Fishing vessel Kilavock, escorted craft
	Dec 27	Cabin cruiser, escorted craft
1992	May 31	Rowing boat, landed 2
	June 6	Fishing vessel, craft brought in
	13	Yacht Windsong, craft brought in
	21	Motor yacht Kamiko, saved craft and 2
	23	Yacht Constance, craft brought in
	July 2	Yacht Islandia, escorted craft
	6	Fishing vessel Unity, gave help
	16	Creel boat Girl Sara, craft brought in
	Aug 5	Inflatable dinghy. saved craft
	Nov 12	Yacht Hobo, saved craft and 1
1993	Jan 16	Sea King helicopter, gave help
	Apr 9	Fishing boat Fisher Lad, craft brought in
	25	Fishing boat Sharoba, gave help
	May 1	Yacht Sara Sian, craft brought in
	July 8	Yacht Isle of Rhona, craft brought in
	15	Yacht Cruisader, gave help
	16	Motor boat Brian MM, craft brought in
	Aug 8	Fishing boat Rochomie, craft brought in
	20	Yacht Double Scotch, landed an ill crewman
	Sep 27	Small power boat, escorted craft
	Oct 11	Fishing boat Wayndalia, craft brought in
	Dec 29	Tug and barge, craft brought in
1994	Feb 3	Windsurfer, person recovered
	June 19	Fishing boat Honey Bee, 2 and craft brought in
	July 10	Yacht Emo Ymeni, 2 persons and craft brought in
	22	Fishing boat, 1 person and craft brought in
	Sep 4	Fishing boat Liberty, 1 person and craft brought in
	21	Fishing boat Integrity, 2 persons and craft brought in
	Nov 5	Fishing vessel Active in tow of fishing vessel My Way, escorted vessels
1995	Feb 12	Fishing vessel Brilliant, landed 2 & craft brought in
	Mar 5	Fishing boat Brilliant, saved boat and 2

Edith Emilie Relief Lifeboat

	Apr 29	Fishing boat Incentive, 2 persons & craft brought in
	29	Motor boat Cara-Mia-Mine, 2 persons and craft brought in
	May 12	Yacht Fung Su, 2 persons and craft brought in
	16	RAF Nimrod Aircraft, recovered wreckage
	27	Yacht, saved boat
	June 25	Yacht Vanagis, gave help
	July 6	Cabin cruiser Alley Cat, 4 persons, craft brought in

Charles Brown Lifeboat

	Aug 3	Cabin cruiser Alley Cat, 3 persons and craft brought in
	17	Fishing vessel Moray Adventurer, 6 persons and craft brought in
	19	Yacht Little Tern, 1 person landed and craft brought in
	23	Yacht Sandgroper, 2 persons & craft brought in
	Nov 8	Cabin cruiser Cockenzie Queen, escorted boat
	28	Fishing vessel Steadfast, saved vessel and 3
1996	Apr 29	Fishing vessel, craft brought in
	May 16	Fishing vessel Hebridean, of Buckie, 4 persons and craft brought in
	June 8	Fishing vessel, landed 2 and craft brought in
	18	Fishing vessel Serene, gave help – 6 persons and craft brought in
	22	Fishing boat Guillemot, of Buckie, saved craft & 2
	July 19	Youth fallen from cliff, gave help
	Aug 9	Motor boat Hebridean, landed 5 & craft brought in
	17	Person in the water in difficulty, saved 1
	22	Speedboat Budweizer, landed 2 & craft brought in
	25	Man on ladder on harbour wall, gave help
	Sep 12	Yacht Northward of Clyde, gave help – 4 persons and craft brought in
	18	Jaguar aircraft crashed, recovered wreckage
	Nov 2	Motor boat, saved craft
1997	Jan 11	Injured man on fishing vessel Moray Explorer, landed injured man and craft brought in
	Apr 8	Motor boat Hebridean, 5 and craft brought in
	May 10	Yacht Dalriada, 2 persons and craft brought in
	June 7	Speedboat Crescendo, 2 persons & craft brought in
	15	Fishing vessel Kedana, gave help
	28	Fishing vessel Alison Kay, stood by craft
	July 18	Yacht Ovation, saved craft and 1
	23	Fishing vessel Star of Bethlehem, 6 persons and craft brought in
	28	Fishing vessel Star of Bethlehem, 3 persons and craft brought in
	Aug 12	Fishing vessel Star of Bethlehem, saved craft & 3
	31	Fishing vessel Fragrant Rose, landed 4 and craft brought in
	Sep 3	Yacht Ester Jensen, gave help
	Nov 3	Fishing vessel Handy Billy, 1 and craft brought in
	Dec 2	Fishing vessel Flowing Stream, 5 persons and craft brought in
		Fishing vessel Mary Elspeth, saved craft and 4
1998	Feb 6	Cargo vessel Oakland, gave help [with Relief LB]
	7	Cargo vessel Oakland, gave help
	Mar 22	Motor boat, 1 person and craft brought in
	May 3	Cabin cruiser Carray, landed 1, craft brought in
	July 2	Yacht Saskia II, 1 person and craft brought in
	20	Speedboat, 3 persons and craft brought in
	30	Fishing vessel Constancy, landed a body & saved 1
	Aug 6	Missing man, landed a body

Snolda Relief Lifeboat

	Sep 26	Yacht Foam, landed 1 and craft brought in
	Oct 20	Survey vessel Talisman, landed 2, craft brought in
	Nov 24	Wreckage, recovered wreckage

Charles Brown Lifeboat

1999	Apr 2	Yacht Seawind, landed 3 and craft brought in
	15	RN coastal training craft HMS Archer, escorted
	20	Fishing vessel Arcturus, gave help

	Apr 27	Fishing vessel Stormer, escorted craft
	June 23	Ordnance in sea, gave help
	25	Fishing vessel Voyager, saved craft and 5
	July 14	Fishing vessel Courage, saved craft and 2
	16	Motor boat Delphis, saved craft
	19	Powered pleasure craft Sunbeam, 2 persons and craft brought in
	Aug 5	Fishing vessel Shona, 1 person & craft brought in
	16	Raft, raft brought in
	23	Fishing boat, 3 persons and craft brought in
2000	Apr 5	Power boat Annie Murray, 2 persons and craft brought in
	July 4	Fishing vessel Hope, 1 person & craft brought in
	5	Diver support craft, saved craft and 4
	Aug 4	Fishing vessel Carolyn Dawn, recovered wreckage

Duchess of Kent Lifeboat

| | 11 | Fishing vessel, saved craft and 1 |

Charles Brown Lifeboat

	Oct 1	Fishing vessel Endeavour, 2 persons and craft brought in
	Dec 30	Recovery of body, landed a body
2001	Apr 2	Fishing vessel Golden Eagle, saved craft and 3
	26	Speedboat, 2 persons and craft brought in
	May 6	Yacht Vanagis, 3 persons & craft brought in
	July 29	Yacht Corrida, landed 2 and craft brought in
		Yacht Old Flame, landed 1 and craft brought in
	Sep 30	Powerboat, saved craft and 2
	Oct 2	Sick diver on board tug Thorax, landed 1

Mickie Salvesen Relief Lifeboat

| 2002 | Feb 13 | Fishing vessel Patsy B, saved vessel and 2 |
| | 27 | Work boat Atair, escorted craft |

Charles Brown Lifeboat

	Apr 16	Raft, saved craft and 1
	May 11	Fishing vessel Lady Grace, saved craft and 2
2003	Feb 20	Fishing vessel Loyal Friend, 1 and craft brought in

William Blannin Lifeboat

	July 20	Three people stranded on rocks, 3 persons brought in
	Aug 2	Yacht, 2 persons and craft brought in
	5	Inflatable dinghy, landed 3 and craft brought in
	Sep 2	Fishing vessel Dalriada, 5 persons and craft brought in
	9	RIB Ketos, 6 persons and craft brought in
	13	Creel boat, 1 persons and craft brought in
	Oct 12	Man overboard yacht Maverick, craft brought in
	24	Yacht Fylla, saved 2
	Nov 3	Fishing vessel Benbola, escorted craft
2004	May 12	Fishing vessel Maridon, 2 and craft brought in
	June 7	Swimmers, landed 2
	30	Fishing vessel, craft brought in

Charles Brown Relief Lifeboat

| | July 15 | Fishing vessel True Vina, 4 and craft brought in |

William Blannin Lifeboat

	Aug 7	Yacht Blink Bonny, 2 persons and craft brought in
	Sep 2	Powered boat Delphis, 4 and craft brought in
	5	Fishing vessel Castlebay, gave help – towed vessel off rocks and unfouled propeller
	Oct 19	Yacht, 2 persons and craft brought in
	Nov 7	Fishing vessel Reaper, escorted craft

Duke of Atholl Relief Lifeboat

| | Dec 12 | Canoe, canoe brought in |
| | 16 | Fishing vessel Golden Eagle, 2 persons brought in |

William Blannin Lifeboat

2005	Jan 10	Powered boat Viking Viper, landed 1
	July 4	Powered boat, 2 people and craft brought in
	July 20	Yacht Saddleworth Moor, 2 people and craft brought in

	Aug 8	Bodyboard, 3 people brought in
	24	Inflatable dinghy, craft brought in
	30	Swimmer, stood by
	Sep 6	Sick fisherman on board fishing vessel, landed 1
	10	Fishing vessel, 1 person and craft brought in
	18	Fishing vessel Argosy, 1 person & craft brought in
	Oct 9	Fishing vessel New Dawn, 5 people and craft brought in
	22	Powered boat Mist Migs, escorted craft
	27	Tenders to HMS Illustrious, fi55ve people and two craft brought in

Osier Relief Lifeboat

| 2006 | Mar 29 | Yacht St Kilda, 1 person and craft brought in |

William Blannin Lifeboat

	Apr 24	Fishing vessel Castlebay, 1 person & craft brought in
	May 4	Fishing vessel Castlebay, 1 person brought in and craft saved
	17	Tug Ala, escorted craft
	July 19	Inflatable dinghy, craft brought in
		Inflatable dinghy, craft brought in
	28	Powered boat Happy Days, 2 persons and craft brought in
	Aug 6	Yacht, 2 persons and craft brought in
	7	Fishing vessel, landed 1 and saved craft
	Sep 19	Fishing vessel Arcana, escorted craft
	Nov 3	Fishing vessel Merlin, 1 person and craft brought in
	7	Fishing vessel Valkirie, 2 and craft brought in
2007	Jan 23	Fishing vessel Blue Sky, 3 persons & craft brought in
	Mar 12	Yacht Stravaiger, 1 person and craft brought in
	25	Canoe, craft brought in
	29	Person stranded, saved 1
	May 6	Yacht Ylva, escorted craft
	19	Fishing vessel Mary Ellen, 2 persons and craft brought in
	25	Yacht Emily, 6 persons and craft brought in
	June 24	Yacht Salker H, escorted craft
	30	Yacht, stood by
	July 14	Yacht Caramba, 1 person and craft brought in
	15	Inflatable dinghy, landed 3 and craft brought in
	22	Fishing vessel Homeland, 2 persons and craft brought in
	Aug 4	Powered boat, 2 persons and craft brought in
	9	Powered boat, escorted craft
	20	Yacht Lune Star, escorted craft
	Sep 4	Yacht Killmore, 2 persons and craft brought in
	16	Powered boat Abijo, landed 2, craft brought in
	28	Fishing vessel, stood by
2008	May 13	Fishing vessel Kai, craft brought in
	June 7	Powered boat Charlotte Rae, three persons and craft brought in
	21	Yacht Spey Breeze, gave help and escorted craft
	27	Powered boat Cinzano 558, 3 persons and craft brought in
	July 4	Fishing vessel Crusty Crab, gave help
	5	Yacht Puffin, 2 persons and craft brought in
	Aug 2	Injured person on rocks, landed 1
	Sep 13	Canoes, four craft brought in
	Oct 7	Oil industry rescue vessel Arcs, 12 persons and craft brought in
2009	Apr 30	Fishing boat, 1 person and craft brought in
	June 21	Dive boat, landed 2, 1 person and craft brought in
	24	Dinghy, 1 person and craft brought in
	25	Fishing boat, 1 person and craft brought in
	July 20	Powered boat, 1 person and craft brought in
	25	Cabin cruiser, 1 person and craft brought in
	Sep 12	Fishing vessel Optimistic, in tow, escorted
	22	Fishing vessel Spring Tide, escorted
	Oct 6	Fishing vessel Discovery, escorted
	Nov 4	Small fishing boat, 1 person and craft brought in
	Dec 15	Yacht Nicari, saved craft and 3

Personnel

Honorary Secretaries

D. Fraser	1860-1863
Alex Bremner	1863-1867
John McDonald	1867-2.1873
William Shirer	2.1873-1874
John Shearer	1874-1884
John Wilson	1884-2.1897
John McNaughton	2.1897-11.1943
John L. McNaughton	11.1943-11.1964
A. Wilson	11.1964-1971
P. Murray	1971-1973
Capt Thomas Garden	1973-1985
John K. Fowlie	1985-2003
Bill Cormack	2003-2008
Joe Herd	2008-

Coxswains

James Gale	1860-70
James Logie	1870-12.1891
Alex Cuthbert	12.1891-1914
John Cowie	1.1914-8.1920
Alex Thomson	8.1920-1.1926
George Smith	1.1926-2.1928
James Goodbrand	2.1928-1.1940
Francis Mair	1.1940-2.1948
William Stewart	2.1948-4.1962
George A. Jappy	4.1962-8.1972
Capt Thomas Garden	8.1972-10.1974
George Wood	10.1974-8.1979
William McDonald*	8.1979-4.1987
John Charles Murray	4.1987-2006
Alan S. Robertson	2006-

Mechanics

Charles Brown	1922-4.1941
Alex Scott	4.1941-4.1943
John Gordon Cole BEM	4.1943-1974
Tony Budge	11.1974-5.1978
William McDonald*	5.1978-4.1987
George Stewart	4.1987-9.1991
George Smith**	16.9.1991-1997
Gordon I. Lawtie***	1997-

Second Coxswains

James Logie	1860-1870
James Lizzis	1.1871-1894
George Cowie	4.1894-10.1902
John Cowie	10.1902-12.13
William Cowie	1.1.1914-?
George A. Jappy	9.1961-3.1962
James Innes	1969-1974
John Charles Murray	1.4.1981-4.1987
Kenny Farquhar	9.1987-3.2001
Alan S. Robertson	3.2001-1.2006
Gordon I. Lawtie***	1.2006-

*Coxswain/Mechanic joint role
**Deputy Second Coxswain/Mechanic from 1.4.1995
***Second Coxswain/Mechanic from 2006

Personnel

▶ Lifeboat Operations Manager Joe Herd. (By courtesy of Buckie RNLI)

▶▶ Deputy Launching Authority (DLA) Adam Robertson (on left), Dr Alison Douglas (Chair of Buckie Station Branch) and Alex Gardiner (DLA). The third DLA is Bill Cormack, who stood down as LOM in 2008 due to work commitments but retained a role with the station as DLA. (Nicholas Leach)

▲ Mechanic Gordon Lawtie in the engine room on board William Blannin. Gordon has clocked up 22 years with the RNLI in a number of differing roles. Originally a crew member, he became full-time Station Mechanic in June 1997. (Cliff Crone)

▲ Coxswain Alan S. Robertson has been a crew member since 1991 after joining aged seventeen. He has held various positions including Second Coxswain and was appointed Coxswain in 2006. He is a self-employed joiner. (Nicholas Leach)